THE

GREAT PIE

Revolt

THE

GREAT PIE

Revolt

A GASTRONOMIC GUIDE TO THE PREMIER LEAGUE AND EFL

JACK PEAT

First published by Pitch Publishing, 2021

Pitch Publishing
A2 Yeoman Gate
Yeoman Way
Worthing
Sussex
BN13 3QZ
www.pitchpublishing.co.uk
info@pitchpublishing.co.uk

A CIP catalogue record is available for this book
from the British Library.

ISBN 978 1 78531 672 2

Typesetting and origination by Pitch Publishing
Printed and bound in India by Replika Press Pvt. Ltd.

Contents

About the author

Football and food fanatic Jack Peat has been addicted to away days from the moment he was old enough to sneak out of the house and follow his beloved club around the country. Now exiled to London, where he edits *The London Economic*, he is a regular contributor to two-time fanzine of the year winner *popular STAND* and contributes to *VICE*, *Huffington Post* and *The Independent*, as well as still making weekend jaunts to discover new grounds and places.

Dedication

For my dad, Chris, who
loves a good pie and
loathes a bad pint.

Introduction: The understated connection between food and football

IT'S THE opening day of the season and an emerald-blue sky meets a rickety train as it snakes out of the dimly lit London Liverpool Street station headed for Southend. Skimming the terrace tops of Mile End, it passes West Ham's doughnut-shaped London Stadium in the old Olympic Park, making a final stop in Stratford before hurtling east towards the tip of the Thames. You can't help but feel a sense of fervent optimism in the air among those who have boarded for the early-August fixture on the coast. After a sun-drenched, football-free summer, filled with tennis, cricket and time with the other half, it feels good to have the old gang back together. The season is young, the possibilities are endless and speculative chitter-chatter reverberates around the carriage. Football is back and, all of a sudden, all is well with the world.

But this season I have decided to do things a little differently. Where usually I would head straight to the ground, to be fed and watered within its proximity, I have decided that the time has come to look further afield. I want to get a sense of a place's identity through the food and drink it produces and make this as big a part of the matchday experience as the match itself. I want to warm my belly with panackelty and stottie in Sunderland, sample the best Shropshire Blue in Shrewsbury, try rag pudding in Oldham and feast on seafood at coastal games. I want to drink local beer, sample small-scale craft ales and even indulge in a glass of wine or two if that's what sets a place apart. I want to eschew the over-the-counter culture that has become the scourge of Football League grounds to develop a deeper appreciation of provenance and the rich diversity that can be found on our tiny island. In short, I want to understand what makes the place I have taken the time to travel to different from the last place, and that requires looking further afield than the confines of the ground.

Just plain awful

I have been a football fan throughout my life, and few things give me more pleasure than a good away day. I enjoy the singing, the camaraderie and the sense of togetherness one gets from travelling to far-flung places with your native townspeople. But one thing I have always found wanting is good food and drink. Sadly, balti pies served out of tin trays, rubbery burgers that cost the best part of a tenner and gravy served in polystyrene cups are a seemingly inevitable part of the football ground catering offering. And while some do it better than others, the reality is that there are few exceptions to the rule.

In 1998 researchers writing for *Colman's Football Food Guide* spent months testing food at the 92 league grounds in England and Wales, plus Wembley. They concluded that the 'taste of the Orient' should be kicked firmly into touch, while summarising the Wembley fare as 'just plain awful'. Even Norwich City, with Delia Smith on the board of directors, didn't get off lightly, landing in a 'disappointing' 61st place out of 93.

The guide noted of Wembley that 'The nation's showcase stadium epitomises everything that's wrong with food at football grounds in this country, an awful, overpriced eating experience', and you would struggle to disagree. Football grounds to this day are hellish experiences for food enthusiasts or even just people with functioning taste buds, and the problem can be summed up by the response of Leyton Orient's club spokesman to the club's lowly position: '

'It's very subjective,' he said. 'Out of 93 clubs, two thirds are exactly the same.' The other third, I would argue, are just a slightly different shade of beige. You may get a somewhat tastier pie at Wigan or a slightly fresher pint at Burton, but by and large the catering at football grounds is pretty much cut from the same cloth. While *Coleman's Guide* set out to do for football what Egon Ronay did for British pub food and motorway service stations, the offering has hardly improved within the last two decades. In many ways, it has got worse.

The great pie revolt

If in '98 the food served in football stadiums was of differing quality, now it is all pretty much the same. Large-scale caterers such as Centerplate, CGC Event, Sodexo and many others ensure most football grounds are tarred with the same nondescript, banal brush. The pies – a staple part of the average football fan's diet – are generally Pukka (the brand, not the Jamie Oliver adjective), and everything else carries a brand that contributes little to the matchday experience but probably a lot to the club's bottom line.

Football clubs, the commercially driven entities that they now are, know that they have a captive audience as soon as a spectator walks through the gate. They are the Ryanair of catering or the juddering food trolley that makes its soulless way down train aisles in the hope that some hapless punter will pay £3 for a sachet of instant coffee. They will happily charge a fiver to hand over a Snickers and a mashed tea bag in hot water because, like being trapped at 30,000 feet in a no-frills tin can en route to Alicante, where else are you going to go?

But for one club, this reality had become all too grim. Mindful that they had once been crowned the FSF's Premier League Away Day of the Year in 2015, Wigan Athletic's fanzine editor and author Martin 'Jimmy' Tarbuck started a petition asking the powers that be at Wigan Athletic and the DW Stadium to stock pies from local company Galloways rather than some bland, generic, petrol station fare. According to Alan Moore of the podcast *The Pie at Night*, it raised a serious point. Following the closure of local supplier Pooles, which had been widely credited with Wigan's rise to fame in the fans' ranks after an illustrious 170-year history, the club brought in Holland's Pies, which despite boasting some provenance (hailing from Baxenden, near Accrington in Lancashire) failed to meet the mark in regards to quality, being more suited to 'truck drivers, travelling salesmen and rubbish indie bands touring the country,' Moore said.

The switch is typical of the generic catering situation that is found across the country, doing little to tantalise the taste buds and damaging the club's role as a focal point of the community. It also highlights a missed opportunity in supporting local businesses, local jobs and strengthening the local economy. The petition bore little fruit as the organiser's cries fell on deaf ears, but the club did agree to honour the town's love of the savoury dish by unveiling a new mascot for the 2019/20 season, a pie named Crusty.

Staggis and Blaggis

But Wigan's rightful place as the UK's pie capital still stands, even if travelling supporters can't get a taste of their proud heritage at the ground. Galloways may have been shunned in favour of the (probably cheaper) Holland's Pies at the DW, but there are several outposts outside of the stadium where their 'quintessential Wigan' meat and potato pie can be sampled, along with the special Staggis (steak and haggis) and Blaggis (black pudding and haggis) pies, which are made using meat supplied by the local butcher, H. Greaves & Son of Skelmersdale.

Those who are a little more adventurous might also consider a trip to Wigan's best-kept secret, the Pepper Lane Pie Shop. The traditional bakers attract custom from far and wide to their quiet corner of Wigan, with queues out of the door often seen from 10am. Formerly known as Gents, the bakery's pies have been tipped as the best in the north-west by one local aficionado, even perhaps England. In his words, 'if tha' can beat it, crack on', but you'd do well; most pies these days do 'now't but give you third-degree burns ont' top o' thy mouth', and when you bite into them and get to the nitty-gritty 'it's now't other than mashed-up slop'. On the other hand, Gents serve up pies that require two hands to eat and use proper meat sauce and real chunks of steak – better than anything Pukka could ever dish up.

And they're not alone. Manze's in Deptford, a stone's throw from The Den in Millwall and The Valley in Charlton, is renowned in south-east London for its pie, mash and liquor offering that spills over the edge of a plate for less than the price of a standard matchday pie. The so-called 'home of pie 'n' mash' has a proud history stretching back to 1902 when the 'godfather', Michele Manze, served up the standard savoury affair alongside eels (jellied or stewed) in authentic surroundings. The recipe hasn't changed until this day and the price has only risen modestly in line with inflation. Rhyming slang is, of course, a must on any visit. A cup of Rosie Lee (tea) goes down very well as the café's standard offering.

A quest for authenticity

Both Manze's and Gents offer a sense of authenticity that no longer exists at football grounds from a gastronomic perspective, which is a real shame given that both lie within spitting distance of their local football clubs. In Millwall, the so-called Bermondsey Beer Mile incorporates some 17 brilliant local breweries with the Fourpure 'base camp' just five minutes away from The Den, where you will find a Carlsberg Ice Bar instead. In Burton, known as the world's most important beer town, they serve typical run-of-the-mill lagers at the Pirelli even though the Beech Hotel has a well-stocked shipping container bar just seven minutes away on foot.

I'll go on. The chance of seeing seafood at Southend's Roots Hall is slim to none even though the ground is moments away from some of the best cockles, mussels and whelks the country has to offer, as is getting your hands on a Hull Pattie at the KCOM or a nice parmo in Middlesbrough's Riverside Stadium. Finding a proper Cornish pasty at Plymouth Argyle's Home Park is impossible, and enjoying a warm oatcake at Port Vale is regrettably not an option either. There are no Eccles cakes in Salford's Moor Lane, laverbread at Swansea's Liberty Stadium or Welsh rarebit at Cardiff City Stadium. Even Everton have stopped handing out the famed mints that were once a staple part of the Goodison Park experience.

But outside of the stadium, these local treats can be found in abundance, which is why this season, on a train headed for Southend, I decided to drag the gang off one stop before the central station and a few nautical miles down the estuary at Leigh-on-Sea, where seafood huts line the shore and punters queue up for lobster, crab, oysters, pickled herring, mussels, potted shrimp, cockles, winkles, smoked eel and more, before carrying it to the outdoor terrace to enjoy with a pint of local ale. The summer heat kissed our necks and arms as we developed T-shirt suntans around our jerseys, baking in the heat without a care in the world. When it got to within half an hour of the game we had to drag ourselves away to watch the very thing we came here to do. But what struck me as we made the short jaunt to Roots Hall is that the outcome wouldn't have mattered. Win or lose, we had made the journey worthwhile before a ball had been kicked, which, as anyone who has faithfully supported lower-league mediocrity will attest, is a desirable proposition.

The Great Pie Revolt is, as such, my quest to make away days more palatable, to marry football and food to create a more rounded, wholesome day out. It is my attempt to make the Football League a gateway into exploring the rich gastronomic map of Britain, to put local cuisine back on the agenda and to eschew the abject uniformity that has swept across stadium canteens. From Cornish pasties served out of the back of a van to panackelty and stottie served in a lighthouse, this is the ultimate companion for eating and drinking your way through the country's professional football pyramid.

Accrington Stanley

> **Fact box**
> Nickname – Stanley
> Colours – Red
> Ground – Crown Ground
> Built in – 1968
> Capacity – 5,450

Introduction

'Accrington Stanley, who are they?' you exclaim in the same high-pitched Scouse accent that is channelled by every football fan in the country at the mere mention of their name. In the 1980s, the Milk Marketing Board deemed the club so obscure they made them the star of a marketing campaign featuring two aspiring footballers who, acting under Ian Rush's guidance, made sure to drink their milk so they didn't end up on the club's books. At the time, Stanley were a non-league outfit and reportedly earned a tidy £10,000 from the ad, which would help sustain them until 2006 when they returned to the Football League. In their first season back, they played and won their first-ever Football League Cup match against former European Cup winners Nottingham Forest. They eventually got knocked out by Watford in a competition many still refer to as the Milk Cup, named after the same Milk Marketing Board that bestowed upon them that most grating turn of phrase.

What to eat and where to eat it

- **Th'Owd Stables**

  Try your hand at taming a 'stallion' at Th'Owd Stables, a micro café based in converted stables at the back of The Abbey Hotel. Three rashers of bacon and three sausages get served alongside the usual full English breakfast mashings, with smaller 'hungry horse' and 'the stables' breakfasts available for those who forgot to wear loose-fitting trousers.

- **The Butty Shop**

  Along with The Butty Box, Proper Butties and Waynes BUTTY VAN, The Butty Shop (the second of the same name) is the jewel in Accrington's butty-shaped crown, serving a range of sandwiches, jacket potatoes and pies. If you're looking for something to set you up for the day, try their 'bin lid', a fluffy bap amply filled with bacon, sausage and eggs.

- **Smokehouse 138**

  Big and bold, Smokehouse 138 is a small American diner a short walk away from the Crown Ground in Clayton-le-Moors. Serving dirty burgers stuffed with slow-cooked meats, ribs and fried chicken, they laugh in the face of the round plate, dispensing their Man vs Food-sized portions on tin trays that speak to your inner carnivore.

What to drink and where to drink it

- **Grants Bar**

  From a run-down, metal-shuttered eyesore to one of the most thriving and burgeoning establishments in the locality, Grants Bar is a beacon of the microbrewing revolution that breathed new life into local pubs across Britain. Serving beer from the local Big Clock Brewery, the tap is a great place to start the day, with pizzas and sharing plates available to help line your stomach.

- **The Crown**

  A handy stop before the game, The Crown is a pub serving a rotating selection of cask ales in a traditional setting. On matchdays, The Little Crown is open in the car park that backs on to the ground, serving a range of butties to wash down with a fresh beer.

- **Thorn Inn**

  Escape to rural Lancashire by taking a short stroll up to where the Tinker Brook meets the Leeds and Liverpool Canal, where you will find a typical Lancastrian pub with a blackened brick exterior and a cosy setup inside. Bank Top's Flat Cap is a regular feature on the taps, with a full complement of Thwaites beer also on show.

AFC Bournemouth

Fact box
Nickname – The Cherries
Colours – Red and black
Ground – Vitality Stadium
Built in – 1910
Capacity – 11,364

Introduction

From pot to plate, you won't find many places with access to crab as fresh as they are in Bournemouth. Set moments away from Dorset's Jurassic Coast where small, beat-up crabbing boats land catches daily, it is not uncommon to find on the menu crab that would have been roaming the rocky seabed just hours before. And you certainly won't be in short supply of places to eat it. On the seafront, WestBeach serves crab 'dressed' by mixing the brown meat found in the main shell and the white meat located in the claws and the body, presenting it in the hollowed shell which doubles as an elegant serving dish. The aptly named Crab at Bournemouth serves crab whole with a dollop of thermidor sauce and garlic butter, while you will find locally sourced Mudeford crab in a sandwich at the Little Pickle Deli not far from the Vitality Stadium. But in this part of the world, eating crab is only half the fun, and if you want the whole Dorset experience you had better remember your coiled string and bait bag before rolling yer kegs up and catching some yerself.

What to eat and where to eat it

- **Little Pickle Deli**

  Established in a bid to bring locally sourced food to the area in a fittingly shabby chic, beach-style setting, Little Pickle Deli is the perfect place to start the day in Bournemouth. The full English features the 'Boscombe banger' and 'Dorset bakehouse' toast, while Mudeford-caught crab sandwiches are available at weekends.

- **Chez Fred**

  Voted the national fish and chip shop of the year in 1991 and lauded by frequent punter Harry Redknapp, Chez Fred is a third-generation chippy in the heart of Bournemouth with ample seating space. Fresh fish is delivered daily from Brixham and Cornwall and can be enjoyed with a mug of tea or perhaps a bottle of Palmers Dorset Gold.

- **Crab at Bournemouth**

  Spicy crab, whole crab, dressed crab and crab salad are just some of the ways to enjoy the local delicacy at the aptly named Crab at Bournemouth. Fresh catches are bought from the local markets in Dorset six days a week, giving you the full pot-to-plate experience.

What to drink and where to drink it

- **Poole Hill Brewery**
  Home of Southbourne Ales, the Victorian-themed Poole Hill Brewery is a highly regarded real ale pub in the heart of Bournemouth. It was voted Dorset's best brewer in 2018, and inside you can take your pick from several bird-themed beers as you kick back in the spacious, turquoise taproom.

- **The Silverback Alehouse**
  Between The Silverback Alehouse and The Micro Moose you'll have a good supply of craft beer on Wimborne Road, a short walk away from the Vitality Stadium. The former specialises in local ales, English wine and hairy creatures of both the human and non-human variety.

- **The Wight Bear**
  Surf's up at local micropub The Wight Bear, where ten taps of keg beer, six cask ales, ten ciders and a good bottle and can selection will have you riding high. Taster flights are also available if you want a little of a lot.

AFC Wimbledon

Fact box
Nicknames – The Dons/The Wombles
Colours – Blue
Ground – Plough Lane
Built in – 2020
Capacity – 9,300

Introduction

Vegan, litter-picking recyclers with a distaste for food waste tend to be associated with the trendier East End parts of London these days, but it wasn't always that way. In the 1970s, out for a walk on the Common, Elisabeth Beresford's young daughter mispronounced 'Wimbledon' as 'Wombledon', thus planting a seed of inspiration in her mother's mind. Shortly afterwards Britain was graced with furious, eco-conscious little creatures who made it their life's work to tidy up after humans as they went about their messy daily business. Living on a diet of plants, fungi and tree products that even the most adventurous hipster might not dare try, they gorged on acorn juice, elm bark casserole and grass bread sandwiches as staple parts of the menu. Fifty years on and vegan cafés lie within walking distance of the park, and a womble known as 'Haydon' makes regular appearances at home games at the reclaimed Plough Lane stadium. As the song goes, he remains 'underground, overground, wombling free'.

THE GREAT PIE REVOLT

What to eat and where to eat it

- **Windmill Tea Rooms**

  Passed down through generations of the same family, the Windmill Tea Rooms on Wimbledon Common offers one of the best breakfasts in the area and by far the best vantage point for spying wombles. Their full English can be enjoyed with black pudding, bubble and fried bread if you so choose.

- **Vegan Express**

  Channel your inner herbivore at the Vegan Express café, a short walk from Plough Lane. A range of vegan burgers, sharing platters and 'tofish and chips' can be found on the menu, as well as a tasty marinated globe artichoke and pizza.

- **Holy Smoke**

  Small, intimate, rustic and full of charm, there are few better places in south London to finish off your day than at the Holy Smoke restaurant. Showcasing a 'contempt for convention', chefs cook seasonal food items flavoured with wine, whisky and woodsmoke.

What to drink and where to drink it

- **The Wimbledon Brewery Company**

  When William Cook started The Wimbledon Brewery in 1832 there were 115 breweries in the London excise district. Today there are roughly the same amount, but their composition has changed drastically over the ages. Thankfully at Wimbledon things have remained much the same, and you can enjoy their ales in a lovely taproom that serves up a variety of fresh cask and keg beer.

- **The Garratt & Gauge**

  Funky and fun, The Garratt & Gauge is a great place to grab a pint or three of several rotating beers that get chalked up on old wooden barrels behind the bar. You will also find a good selection of bottled and canned beers that are worthy of consideration.

- **By The Horns Brewing Co.**

  An idyllic pre- or post-match stop, By The Horns Brewing Co. is a local microbrewery plying its trade in a bright blue industrial unit in Summerstown. Its core range includes West End Pils and Old Smoke Tea Bitter.

Arsenal

Fact box
Nickname – The Gunners
Colours – Red and white
Ground – The Emirates
Built in – 2006
Capacity – 60,704

Introduction

Long before the owners of Wimbledon FC sat down to discuss moving the club 56 miles north to Milton Keynes, a gaggle of workers from the Woolwich Arsenal Armament Factory met in the Royal Oak pub on Christmas Day 1886 and decided to form a football team called Dial Square. They won their opening fixture 6-0 – a feat that would be repeated over a century on in Arsène Wenger's 1,000th game – on a ground ten miles south of their current home. Today The Gunners ply their trade in Highbury, north London, much to the annoyance of local teams Tottenham and Clapton Orient. But it leaves them close to the cosmopolitan borough of Islington, with restaurants, pubs and cafés in abundance, as well as several transport options.

What to eat and where to eat it

- **The Hope Dining Rooms**

  The Hope Dining Rooms, also known as The Hope Workers' Café, is a traditional north London greasy spoon a short stroll away from the Emirates offering set breakfasts at a very reasonable price. Take a pick of seven sets, with the conventional full English fare on offer alongside liver, bubble and a fried slice, served alongside a mug of builder's tea or coffee, any of which will set you back less than a fiver.

- **Piebury Corner**

  Sample the delights of the UK's first-ever 'Pie Deli' at Piebury Corner, which serves a range of mouth-watering 'pie legends' on all home fixtures. Sample the 'Dennis Bergkamp' chicken, ham and leek pie or the 'Lee Dixon' vegetarian balti among many other dishes at its Kings Cross restaurant or at a stall beside Highbury Stadium on matchdays, where the owners set up the first-ever shop in a front garden.

- **Black Axe Mangal**

  Described as a cross between a swish Turkish kebabery and a hard rock music venue, Black Axe Mangal (or BAM, if you prefer) is a loud, fun and boisterous restaurant run by an army of tattooed cooks near Highbury and Islington station. A graffitied wood-fired oven dominates the open kitchen, while the menu celebrates oft-underappreciated cuts of meat such as oxtail and dripping, brisket and ox heart, and lamb offal and pigskin. Places are limited, but there is always a waiting list for walk-ins on the day.

What to drink and where to drink it

- ### The Che Guevara

  The Che Guevara pub, also known as El Comandante, is a South American bar based in a pub formerly known as Lord Palmerston in Holloway. Run by a Bolivian landlord, it is decorated with huge Che Guevara pictures that line the walls. A jukebox spews out Latin music and there is cerveza aplenty for comrades to swill on matchdays when supporters spill out on to the street.

- ### Bank of Friendship

  A must-visit on sunny days, the Bank of Friendship is a small independent pub with a great beer garden and charming bar area serving a range of local and world craft beers alongside a large gin and whisky selection. If you get peckish, you can order delicious pizza directly to the pub from Yard Sale just down the road, which delivers for free.

- ### The Gunners

  Always a big hit with Arsenal fans, The Gunners pub pays homage to the club's armament past, along with its long, illustrious footballing history, with a bar that is cluttered with memorabilia. There are several TV screens for the pre-match build-up and the atmosphere is always on point. If you're lucky, there's also often live music at night, with a wide array of bands taking to the stage.

**With thanks to *The Gooner*

Aston Villa

Fact box
Nickname – The Villa
Colours – Claret and blue
Ground – Villa Park
Built in – 1897
Capacity – 42,749

Introduction

For faggots, see Walsall.

'Whatever happened to Groaty Dick, Kunzle cakes and tripe?' Fionnuala Bourke wrote in the *Birmingham Post & Mail* in 2007. Changing food habits in the Midlands had got her concerned, with a Sainsbury's survey claiming many old-fashioned Black Country dishes could be wiped out within the next 50 years. If you fancy a Chinese takeaway, Italian pizza or Turkish kebab you can have one at your house within the next 30 minutes just by picking up the phone. But try to find a traditional favourite like the Birmingham tripe supper, faggots or groaty pudding and it's a very different story, she noted, with an explosion of food delivery apps serving only to exacerbate the trend. That did not sit well with Richard James, a present-day Faggot Pioneer, who set out to write a book on the traditional treat in a bid to put it back on the menus. But the meal from which he takes his nickname, Grorty Dick, has a more challenging fight for survival on its hands. Unlike its pork companion, a meatball-like mixture of pork offcuts and flavourings, it has a more acquired taste, made from oat husks, leeks, onion stock and cheap cuts of beef. It tends to rear its head in some quarters of Birmingham on Bonfire Night, but sightings elsewhere are sparse.

What to eat and where to eat it

- **Yorks Café – Ikon Gallery**
  For a classic fry-up served *à la pan*, head to Yorks Café in the Ikon Gallery, where a former school has been stripped back to create a modern, stone-clad restaurant. Those needing an early morning pick-up should order the house-roasted coffee; it is a real touch.

- **Edwardian Tea Rooms**
  Based in the Birmingham Museum and Art Gallery. If you are lucky, this is one of the few places in Brum where you might find groaty dick, a shin of beef cooked low and slow with leeks, carrots and groats braised in a rich Midlands ale gravy and served with Brummy bacon cakes.

- **The Bull**
  You will find the best faggots and peas in Birmingham at The Bull pub on Price Street in the Gun Quarter. Known as the 'country pub in the city', you will get a real taste for the Black Country here.

What to drink and where to drink it

- **Gunmakers Arms**

  Brewery pub the Gunmakers Arms is the perfect place to become acquainted with Birmingham on any given Saturday afternoon, located en route from the city centre to Aston. Two Towers Brewery is at the back of the pub, providing fresh pints of Complete Muppetry, Chamberlain Pale and Bhacker Ackhams.

- **Burning Soul Brewing Co.**

  Burning Soul Brewing Co. and taproom can be found in an industrial estate just a three-minute walk from Snow Hill station outside of the famed Jewellery Quarter. You'll often find a good crowd of people in this unlikely drinking spot knocking back pints of Life on Mars, Ice Cream Pale and Darkness my Old Friend.

- **Tilt**

  For craft beer, speciality coffee and pinball machines, there really is no better place in the country than Tilt. With no fewer than 19 pinball machines to choose from, you can re-engage your retro self as you sip on a large selection of carefully curated beers.

Barnsley

Fact box
Nickname – The Tykes
Colours – Red
Ground – Oakwell
Built in – 1887
Capacity – 23,287

Introduction

If I had one criticism of lamb chops it would be that, on the whole, they are never really big enough. Taken individually from the ribs of the lamb, they are incredibly delicious and tender but can often leave you feeling unfulfilled and hungry for more as you gnaw away at the bone. But back in 1849, fed up with paltry portions after a hard day at the market, a group of farmers dining in Barnsley's Kings Head Hotel ordered lamb. Not a mere chump, but a double-loin cut across the saddle, creating a hearty meal befitting the sweat and toil of their labours in Yorkshire's rugged fields. In doing so, they made the Barnsley chop, which rose to prominence across the country and can now be found in many fine dining establishments, most famously at chef James Mackenzie's Michelin-starred Pipe and Glass Inn, where he serves it with devilled kidneys, and nettle and mint sauce.

What to eat and where to eat it

- **Passion Food Restaurant**

  You will find the best breakfast in Barnsley a short walk away from the Interchange at Passion Food Restaurant, where a coiled Cumberland sausage takes pride of place on the plate next to crispy black pudding, bacon, beans, mushrooms and a freshly made cup of ground coffee.

- **8oz Burger Co.**

  With views of Oakwell from the top of the street, the 8oz Burger Co. is an ideal place to stop on the way to the ground or your return, cooking up juicy burgers, ribs, loaded fries and chicken. Tackle the 'farmyard' if you feel up to it with a standard 8oz beef patty served with chicken breast, pulled pork and shredded brisket.

- **Beatson House Restaurant**

  These days you will have to travel a little to find the authentic Barnsley chop. Beatson House in Cawthorne still serves the cut of the meat, which was introduced over eight decades ago, cooking it exceptionally slowly for the best results. Be sure to order ahead if you want to get your hands on one.

What to drink and where to drink it

- **The Old No 7**
  Billed as a real ale lover's paradise in the heart of Barnsley, The Old No 7 is a traditional pub and beer emporium serving the full range from Acorn Brewery as well as keeping guest places for Crouch Vale, Dark Star and Ossett breweries. Pull up a pew in the long main bar or head downstairs to the cellar bar.

- **George and Dragon**
  Knock back a Barnsley Bitter and Yorkshire Pride at the George and Dragon, where a good selection of Acorn brews are served alongside craft beers from Magic Rock and the like. You will also find a spacious beer garden out back for the warm days.

- **Jolly Tap on the Arcade**
  A real ale café in Barnsley's historic arcade, on matchdays the Jolly Tap is a popular haunt among football fans who often spill out on to the shopping precinct, pint in hand. Try a Yorkshire Pale Ale, aka YPA, from Jolly Boys' Brewery with a Percy Turner pork pie.

Barrow

Fact box
Nickname – The Bluebirds
Colours – Blue
Ground – Holker Street
Built in – 1909
Capacity – 5,045

Introduction

Dave Myers and Martin Tarbuck have both written books on pies. The former, as one half of the Hairy Bikers, from a cooking perspective and the latter from an eating perspective. But both came to the same conclusion: that the best pie shop in the country isn't to be found in Wigan, or Melton Mowbray, or even the East End of London, but in the humble Cumbrian town of Barrow-in-Furness at Green's Bakers. For it is there that after sampling hundreds of baked delicacies across a two-year odyssey Tarbuck cried out, 'Yes! Yes! Yes! This is what I've been searching for!' as he sank his teeth into a delicious meat and potato creation. It was the very pie that Myers would eat as a child, having been born nearby, and he still does whenever he returns. Recalling his perfect pie moment in *The Ultimate Pie Bible from the Kings of Pies*, Myers points to 'the smell of the freshly baked pies from the corner shop in Barrow', a scent that draws many hungry punters daily who queue down Jarrow Street to get a taste. Succulent meat with a hint of pepperiness and chunky potato is clothed in pastry that is both delicate and crisp, yet sturdy enough to hold the substantial filling. Any trip to Barrow is not complete without sampling one, and then stuffing your backpack with several more for the journey home.

What to eat and where to eat it

- **Peace and Loaf Bakehouse**
  Find some of the best bread this side of the Irish Sea at Peace and Loaf Bakehouse, now housed in the Trinity Enterprise Centre. Bacon sarnies served on brioche buns using local produce from Sillfield Farm are an excellent way to kick off the day. Toasties and baked goods are also usually stacked on the counter.

- **Green's Bakers**
  Green's Bakers may cut a humble figure, occupying a small shop at the end of a row of terraced houses on Jarrow Street, but it is anything but. Considered to make one of the best pies in Britain by *Life of Pies* author Martin Tarbuck, it produces a range of baked goods, but its meat and potato creation is the one that was deemed to be 'piefection'.

- **deli.sh**
  The new kid on the block but one that is increasing in popularity, deli.sh on Crellin Street produces a solid core of award-winning pies that hold their own in a competitive field. But it excels with the more inventive creations, such as a pork and cider casserole pie with suet dumplings on top.

What to drink and where to drink it

- **The King's Arms**

  Burrowed away in the Barrow suburb of Hawcoat, The King's Arms is a superb real ale pub featuring a regular line-up of Cumbrian brewers on tap. Expect ales from Keswick, Bowness Bay, Kirkby Lonsdale and elsewhere to be chalked up beside the bar.

- **White Lion**

  Owned by the Robinsons Brewery of Stockport, the White Lion is a charming pub that is never short of a good supply of guest ales to complement Dizzy Blonde and Unicorn staples. Beers from the Lakes usually get a good showing. Try the Loweswater Gold if it's on.

- **Duke of Edinburgh**

  There's no better place to finish up after a long day in Barrow than with your feet up in front of a roaring fire at the Duke of Edinburgh. There are usually up to eight cask beers to try before you head off home. A wee tipple from Lancaster Brewery isn't a bad shout.

Birmingham City

Fact box
Nickname – The Blues
Colours – Blue
Ground – St Andrew's
Built in – 1906
Capacity – 29,409

Introduction

The Anglicisation of Indian food is well documented in Britain, with people often quick to point out that the nation's favourite dish – the chicken tikka masala – is actually a Glaswegian creation. Such claims are disputed, but one thing we know for sure is that the dish known as balti was invented in Birmingham in the 1970s and it remains a big part of the UK's second city to this day. Unlike the tikka masala, its conception was less to do with taste and more to do with time, after restaurant owners of the Pakistani community in Sparkbrook, keen to cash in on an increasing fondness for Asian cuisines in the local area, realised they required curries to be cooked more quickly than in their native Mirpur. They developed dishes they could prepare and serve in steel dishes, naming them after the Hindi word 'balty', meaning 'bucket'. As of 2020, there were almost 50 restaurants located in the area of Birmingham known as the Balti Triangle, including the esteemed Adil's and Shabab. The restaurateurs form the Birmingham Balti Association, and among other things, campaign to give the dish protected status alongside such regional classics as the Cornish pasty and Stilton blue cheese. Their efforts, alas, have so far been unsuccessful, but we can at least doff our caps to them in these pages and make sure to pay a visit on any given away day.

What to eat and where to eat it

- **The English Breakfast Club**
  Hot food, mugs of tea and craft beer signs welcome you on arrival to one of Birmingham's premier breakfast joints, where you will find a good selection of food choices alongside a stonking good full English.

- **Adil's**
  Finding a good curry in Birmingham's Balti Triangle is like shooting fish in a barrel, but there is no better place to start than at the restaurant considered to be the 'daddy of the balti', Adil's of Stoney Lane. Its owner Mohammed Arif is widely credited for inventing the dish in the '70s.

- **Shabab**
  Shabab owner Zafar Hussain literally wrote the book on how to cook a balti after welcoming Hairy Bikers Si King and Dave Myers to his restaurant in 2016. You will find up to 20 balti dishes to choose from during your visit.

What to drink and where to drink it

- **The Bull's Head**

  Cask ales, craft beers, Birmingham heritage and bartenders in Peaky Blinders attire will provide you with the full Brummy experience on Bishopsgate Street. The Bull's Head serves the full range from Davenports Brewery as well as from historic Midlands brewer Dares.

- **Dig Brew Co.**

  Digbeth craft brewers Dig Brew Co. operates out of a splendid taproom on River Street, halfway between New Street station and St Andrew's. Try its California fruit smoothie sour and barrel-aged imperial stout, both of which come with wax seals.

- **KILDER**

  Craft beer emporium KILDER is the perfect place to experience choice paralysis, with just shy of 20 craft ales on tap and an extensive range of cans and bottles. All beers are chalked up behind the bar, leaving you staring into the abyss as the bartender grows impatient.

Blackburn Rovers

Fact box
Nickname – Rovers
Colours – Blue and white
Ground – Ewood Park
Built in – 1882
Capacity – 31,367

Introduction

For every Sheikh Mansour there has always been a Venky's Chicken, or so the saying goes in the Lancastrian town of Blackburn, which lies just 25 miles north of the Etihad Stadium. Over the years clubs with dreams of making the big time have found the lure of overseas cash hard to pass up after Russian, Emirati, Thai and American billionaires made the top flight a competition of means above anything else. But things don't always work out as you want. After a near-total buyout by an Indian poultry company in 2010, Blackburn Rovers – winners of the Premier League in 1995 – have struggled to re-enact the glory years, dropping into League One in 2017 and posting mid-table positions since. A video, released on behalf of Venky's in 2011, came to symbolise the demise, with the starting XI filmed chowing down on nine plates of chicken before a game. 'Just like that, memories of Shearer and Sutton terrorising defences were gone,' one fan wrote shortly after. A bemused David Dunn and brightly coloured pieces of meat were all that was left in their place.

What to eat and where to eat it

- **Checks & Greys**

  Taking their name from the traditional weaving pattern that once made Blackburn world-famous, Checks & Greys is an independently run café situated in the modern cloisters of the cathedral. Sample local black pudding and Ribble Valley sausages as part of its 'full Lancashire breakfast', or head back a little later on to try Blackburn Cathedral's own Cathedra Gin over ice with a crisp tonic.

- **Leavers Bakery**

  Packed full of meat, delicately encased in pastry and infinitely better than anything you'll get in the football ground, Leavers Bakery pies are widely regarded among locals as being the best in Lancashire. The meat and potato pie is its trademark and comes with their signature hole in the top. The butter pie is also a must on a visit to the West Pennine Moors.

- **Calypso Restaurant**

  Otherwise known as The Riversiders, Blackburn once relied on its waterways as an essential component of its 19th-century industrial growth. You can rediscover its past in the warmth of the Calypso Restaurant on the Wharf, a hearty Caribbean joint serving authentic dishes seasoned with 'a little bit o' dis and a little bit o' dat'.

What to drink and where to drink it

- **The Drummer's Arms**

  Blackburn's first micropub, The Drummer's Arms, cuts the figure of a pub that has been on the scene for decades, despite only being opened in 2016. A dark exterior and exposed wood-beam interior reflect the town's persona, particularly as it is wedged next to the historic landmark Cotton Exchange building.

- **Navigation Inn**

  The Navigation Inn marries two things that Blackburn holds dear to its heart: the Leeds and Liverpool Canal and Thwaites Brewery. Lying on the waterway banks on a cobblestone road, the pub is steeped in history and is well worth making a detour for, come rain or shine.

- **The Black Bull/Three Bs**

  Described as a 'haven on the hill', The Black Bull is a classic pub with an on-site microbrewery boasting suburb views across the West Pennine Moors, over the Ribble Valley and as far as the Blackpool Tower for those with good vision. On a summer's day there is no better place in the world to drink good local ale than in the Bull. Take a taxi there and roll yourself back if you want my advice.

Blackpool

Fact box
Nickname – The Seasiders
Colours – Orange
Ground – Bloomfield Road
Built in – 1899
Capacity – 17,338

Introduction

Although the origins of seaside rock are contested, one thing that is certain is that Blackpool played a significant role in elevating it into the hearts of British holidaymakers everywhere. The earliest form of rock is said to have come from the south coast at the Rock Fair in Hastings during the 19th century, when sugar was abundant and inexpensive. Ben Bullock, an ex-miner from Burnley, is said to have evolved the idea into the brightly coloured, lettered candy sticks we are familiar with today, at his Yorkshire-based sweet factory after visiting Blackpool on holiday. Others believe the credit should go to a Victorian character who goes by the name of 'Dynamite Dick', who borrowed the idea from Rock Fair and added lettering to make the design his own. Regardless, no trip to the once-popular holiday resort is complete without leaving with a long stick of boiled sugar in your pocket.

What to eat and where to eat it

- **Promenade Café**

  For most passengers disembarking from the train at Blackpool North, their next steps consist of the quickest and most direct route to the seaside. A long stretch of beach, promenade and old-fashioned tram lines lie within a few minutes' walk of the station, with a first-rate breakfast to be had at the Promenade Café on Cocker Square.

- **Coronation Rock**

  With the capacity to create over 100,000 sticks of rock candy per day, the Coronation Rock factory stands as one of the last remaining powerhouses of seaside confectionery in the country. Supplying sweet stands up and down the coast with the world-famous hard candy cane, the traditional peppermint is a must on any visit to Blackpool. However, you can try marmite, cheese and tomato pizza and even alcoholic ones if you feel up to it.

- **The Cottage**

  Widely regarded as the best fish and chips in the town, The Cottage is a historic and popular restaurant dating back to the 1920s. Featured in Rick Stein's *Seafood Lovers' Guide*, the walls are covered with pictures of celebrities who have enjoyed the wide range of fresh fish, famous home-cut chips and fresh local peas, including Freddie Flintoff, Lenny Henry, Dawn French, Status Quo and even John Major.

What to drink and where to drink it

- **The Brew Room**

  The best place for a Blackpool Blonde, The Brew Room proudly stands as the town's first brewery pub, serving local ales from West Coast Rock, Cross Bay and Mobberley Brewhouse. Indulge in a Golden Mile and Tangerine Dream while you are there; just be careful not to walk out like a Wonky Donkey when time is called at the bar.

- **Albert's Ale Micropub**

  Home to almost 300 hotels, Blackpool certainly has no shortage of places to stay. Albert Road, which stretches a mere few hundred feet, is home to at least ten per cent of them, with its namesake lodgings housing a surprisingly good real ale pub. Expect ales from Bowland Brewery, the Big Bog and Avid.

- **The Galleon Bar**

  Win, lose or draw, there's no better place to end a day in Blackpool than at The Galleon Bar. Musical instruments adorn the room, and pictures of rock icons and retro pop memorabilia can be found in abundance. Live music is generally found in some form, ranging from trained musicians to tipsy karaoke singers.

Bolton Wanderers

Fact box
Nickname – The Trotters
Colours – White
Ground – University of Bolton Stadium
Built in – 1997
Capacity – 28,723

Introduction

Despite falling out of favour with fans, the Bolton Wanderers traditional nickname harks back to when pig or sheep trotters were a popular local delicacy that, it has been claimed, was even fed to the team as part of their pre-match meal. A butcher based near the former stadium of Burnden Park used to pile them up in his shop window before matchdays, providing much-needed sustenance on cold Lancastrian afternoons. Rumour also has it that the club might have acquired the nickname because its base at Pike's Lane was situated next to a pigsty, causing players to 'trot' through the pig pens to retrieve the ball if it went over the fence. Today, lesser-known cuts of meat can be picked up at Bolton Market, where Karl's Butchers sells trotters, offal, tripe and pig heads among other things.

What to eat and where to eat it

- **Odessa Café**

  Experience the best of Bolton at Odessa Café, where fresh and local produce can be found in abundance within a cosy café setting. Along with a range of breakfasts, baguettes, jackets and barms, you can browse the deli counter, where a range of cooked meats, local cheeses and even homemade chutneys and pickles are on display. You can even get a bag of traditional sweets to take away and smuggle into the ground.

- **Ye Olde Pastie Shoppe**

  Find stacks of pies laid out enticingly in Ye Olde Pastie Shoppe's window off the cobblestone street of Churchgate. Established in 1667, it has become something of an institution in the town, serving local delicacies such as pasties, pea soup and whist pies filled with spiced-salt meat and jelly. Those with a sweet tooth should try their wimberry pie, also known as 'mucky mouth pie'. You'll find out why after a few hearty mouthfuls.

- **Nkono**

  Widely regarded as the most outstanding goalkeeper Africa ever produced, Tommy N'Kono is a former Cameroonian international who allegedly inspired a young Gianluigi Buffon to switch position from midfielder to goalkeeper after his impressive performance at Italia 90. Today a small market stall in Bolton Market pays tribute to the star, serving straight talkin', lip smackin', street eatin' African food.

What to drink and where to drink it

- **The Ale House**

  Home to Bank Top Brewery, The Ale House in Horwich is a proper Lancastrian pub serving a range of beers from Bolton's oldest and most acclaimed brewery. Doff your cap to a Flat Cap bitter or indulge in a Pavilion Pale Ale named after the picturesque Grade II-listed tennis pavilion the brewery is now housed in.

- **Blackedge**

  An amalgamation of the Blackrod and Edgworth villages on the outskirts of Bolton, Blackedge Brewery is an award-winning microbrewery at the heart of the small independent brewing community in the north-west. The bar is located directly above the brewery, fusing traditional and industrial furnishings to create a perfect pre-match drinking spot.

- **Ye Olde Man & Scythe**

  One of the ten oldest public houses in Britain, Ye Olde Man & Scythe is a renowned local boozer and the historic neighbour of Ye Olde Pastie Shoppe on Churchgate. Dating back to the 13th century, it has a charming interior with vaulted cellars, exposed wooden beams and even its very own ghost in residence.

Bradford City

Fact box
Nickname – The Bantams
Colours – Claret and amber
Ground – Valley Parade
Built in – 1886
Capacity – 25,136

Introduction

Although the origins of Bradford City's signature claret and amber kit are disputed, it has been widely claimed that they are probably based on the resemblance to the colours of either wine and beer or rhubarb and custard. The city once formed part of Yorkshire's Rhubarb Triangle, famed for producing 'early forced' rhubarb, and the local produce would have provided a welcome warm pudding after a cold winter's fixture. Today Bradford has a proud culinary scene that has evolved to incorporate a compelling mix of traditional and international cuisine. Its reputation for Asian food is well established and it frequently takes the mantle of the Curry Capital of the UK. But be sure not to overlook its real ale heritage, with stunning beers from Timothy Taylor's, Saltaire Brewery and Bingley Brewery all keeping the city well watered.

What to eat and where to eat it

- **Sultan Restaurant**

  A stone's throw away from Valley Parade, the Sultan Restaurant is widely regarded as the best curry house in the UK's Curry Capital. It boasts an intriguing menu that isn't beholden to the usual Anglo-Indian staples, you are treated to an authentic experience and an economical one at that. Be sure to try the chicken karahi, which is served with salad, a mint yoghurt dip and warm, fluffy, homemade chapatis.

- **PIND Restaurant**

  Dubbed 'The Taste of Lahore', PIND Restaurant serves a traditional Pakistani fare in what looks like a warehouse-cum-temple conversion. A complete list of Lahore karahis come in half- or full-kilo portions (always err on the side of caution). Still, the handi is deserving of serious consideration, with a range of dishes cooked in clay pots to create a wonderful fusion of flavour. The palak gosht handi is a must-try here.

- **The Record Café**

  A treat for food and music lovers alike, The Record Café is an independent record shop, real ale bar and charcuterie counter rolled into one. Winner of Bradford CAMRA Pub of the Year in 2017 and 2019, its reputation is well established on the drinks front, with a large selection of local beers to choose from. But the food is equally good, with a selection of ham, salami and cheese to enjoy along with a house speciality, the 'pulpo a feira', mouth-watering pieces of marinated octopus served on ciabatta.

What to drink and where to drink it

- **The Fighting Cock**

  Hidden among Bradford's industrial back streets, The Fighting Cock has the feel of an open-air museum with Romany-style frontage and a bare-board interior. The beers of the day are chalked up above a log burner with a healthy selection of local breweries on show. Expect Timothy Taylor's, Theakstons and Salamander ales served in a traditional spit and sawdust setting.

- **Sunbridgewells**

  Take a walk back in time in Bradford's historic tunnels, which have in turn served as prison cells, an air raid shelter and a soul club over time. The subterranean maze of bars, shops and eateries works as a perfect pre- or post-match boozer with a good range of Saltaire beer on at a really affordable price. It's a five-minute walk from either Foster Square or Bradford Interchange.

- **The Sparrow Bier Café**

  Lovers of diverse beer styles will find a friendly home at The Sparrow Bier Café located near the PIND Restaurant and The Record Café. A range of local brews is served alongside bottled craft beer from the UK, Belgium and USA to name a few. They also have a range of bar snacks such as meat and cheese platters and locally sourced pies to pick from.

** With thanks to George Peat and colleagues

Brentford

Introduction

Home to Brentford FC from the turn of the 20th century, Griffin Park was well known in football circles not only for being home to a small double-decker stand dubbed the 'Wendy House' but also for being the only football ground in England to have a pub on each corner. The New Inn on Ealing Road was a favourite with travelling fans due to its proximity to the away end, but The Princess Royal, Royal Oak and The Griffin were all once decent calling points for those wanting to complete the set. Today the club is based next to Kew Bridge, where you will find a good complement of drinking houses still remaining, with local brewery Fuller's a brief walk away in Chiswick.

What to eat and where to eat it

- **Verdict Bakery**

  Kick off the day with a 'guilty breakfast' at Brentford's old courthouse, which is now home to Verdict Bakery. The distinctive building houses a famous clock tower built in 1755 by the local clockmaker, John Jullion. Today, produce from local butchers Macken Brothers can be enjoyed with all the trimmings in a fine full English, which is best enjoyed alongside a plate of toast and preserves.

- **Siracusa**

  Enjoy views across the Grand Union Canal at Siracusa, where you can enjoy antipasti al fresco or a cosy pasta dish in the heart of the renovated lock. A robust small plate selection includes deep-fried goat cheese and sun-dried tomato, buffalo mozzarella with aubergine croquettes and Italian cured meats served with Sardinian flatbread. Its pizza menu is also popular with the locals.

- **Man vs Food**

  See if you're good for the hall of fame or the wall of shame at the belly-busting food extravaganza that is Man vs Food on Syon Lane. Can you finish 30 wings, a metre-long hot dog or three full racks of pork ribs in 30 minutes? You will win an MVF T-shirt, your money back and a photo on the wall if you do, with a food coma assured either way.

What to drink and where to drink it

- **Express Tavern**

  Find a range of Big Smoke beer on tap at the Express Tavern, situated a stone's throw from Kew Bridge station and the new Community Stadium. The small bar and a series of partitioned rooms are traditionally decorated, with ample space to be found in the beer garden which backs on to the ground.

- **The Mawson Arms**

  Standing proudly next to the famous Fuller's Griffin Brewery is The Mawson Arms, a Grade II-listed public house serving up the freshest London Pride on the market. Once home to 18th-century poet Alexander Pope, the building was previously named the Fox & Dogs, then the Fox & Hounds until 1898, when it took on the moniker of Thomas Mawson, the first brewer on the site in the late 17th century.

- **The Griffin**

  Once part of the quartet of corner-flag pubs, The Griffin remains a worthy pit stop just a short walk away from the new ground. With distinctive Fuller's branding outside and a cosy, carpeted interior, it is an archetypal London pub, which is perhaps why it featured in the football film *Green Street* despite being in no way related to Chelsea or West Ham.

Brighton & Hove Albion

Introduction

Home to one of the highest number of restaurants per head and the highest density of pubs per square mile in the country, it is a wonder chain restaurants even bother with Brighton and Hove. Once the hub of the old fishing town Brighthelmstone, the Lanes is packed to the rafters with funky cafés, quirky dining spots and independent boozers that stand out on its narrow, twisting alleyways. And that isn't the half of it. Such is the proliferation of vegan restaurants, coffee shops, tattoo studios, vintage boutiques and record stores that the city was ranked number one in the world on a 'hipster index', ahead of Portland, Salt Lake City and Seattle in the US. Picking a good place to eat and drink is a little like shooting fish in a barrel, so long as the barrel is ethically sourced and has been handcrafted with love, etcetera.

What to eat and where to eat it

- **Sugardough**

  On the seafront, a short walk from Hove Station lies the Sugardough bakery, which should be visited for two reasons: fresh coffee and their 'breakfast Danish' – egg, bacon and black pudding encased in pastry. Devour with a hot drink on the pebble beach.

- **Trollburger**

  Organic dirty burgers served out of a shed by a pub near Brighton train station. Need I say more? Well, the 'filthy beast', 'imperial armageddon' and 'troll's stinky breath' are among the options, all of which should be consumed with a big pile of napkins handy.

- **The Coal Shed Restaurant**

  'If you haven't eaten a coal-based meal have you really visited Brighton?' you might ask, but if charcoal-activated vegan croissants aren't your thing, you could do a lot worse than finish your day at The Coal Shed Restaurant. Seasonal, local ingredients are expertly cooked over coal, with fish and steak taking pride of place on the menu.

What to drink and where to drink it

- **John Harvey Tavern**

  For those journeying down to Brighton and Hove on the train, a stop off in Lewes, one stop before Falmer, the station closest to the ground, is worth considering. You will find a rustic old pub serving the beers of John Harvey on the River Ouse banks.

- **Brighton Beer Dispensary**

  A homespun pub nestled at the end of a row of terraced housing in the city, the Brighton Beer Dispensary has a warm and welcoming feel with intimate seating indoors and out. Regular rotating beers get chalked up behind the bar, with up to nine keg and five cask beers to choose from.

- **Old Tree Brewery**

  Head down to the Old Tree Brewhouse Café for an experience unlike any other. Combining brewing and gardening with forest farming and fermentation, this ethical hideout specialises in kombucha brewing, giving you a much-needed health boost after a long day out.

Bristol City

Fact box
Nickname – The Robins
Colours – Red
Ground – Ashton Gate
Built in – 1887
Capacity – 27,000

Introduction

Commonly known as the Cider Army, Bristol City has a connection to the local West Country brew that stretches back generations. Their anthem, 'One for the Bristol City', was written by self-titled 'Scrumpy and Western' band The Wurzels, who are more commonly known for their hits 'The Combine Harvester' and 'I am a Cider Drinker', and their mascot, Scrumpy the Robin, also gives a proud nod to the rough and at times lethal brew. On particularly merry days, the anthem 'Drink Up thee Cider' can be heard reverberating around Ashton Gate, which boasts that they can 'do Rovers over' and 'still pour cider in thee jar', a fate many of their rivals are often only too happy to succumb to.

What to eat and where to eat it

- **Clark's Pies**

  Dating back to the start of the 20th century, Clark's Pies is a popular bakery serving time-honoured savoury treats right out of its bakehouse on North Street. Its traditional pie is famous for its pastry, which is thick enough to eat without a foil tray and is made with the same ingredients as it was first made from over a hundred years ago: beef, ox kidneys, potatoes, onions and a special gravy. The steak and ale pie is also worth a nod, made with beer sourced directly from the Bristol Beer Factory.

- **El Rincón**

  Small and unassuming, El Rincón is a tiny tapas bar serving small plates, beer and cider, a short walk away from Ashton Gate stadium. Split boquerones, lomo and patatas bravas in the exposed brick bar over a range of Spanish bottles including Mahou, Cruzcampo and Alhambra Reserva. If you fancy something stronger, a list of long drinks is also available, including the classic Andalucian refresher Rebujito Fino y Sprite and the Basque country quencher Kalimotxo (Coca-Cola and red wine).

- **Tobacco Factory**

  Strike a light for independents at the Tobacco Factory, a multipurpose building that became home to a raft of cafés, markets and meeting spaces when the grounds of the old Imperial Tobacco site were saved from demolition by architect George Ferguson. The Yard Kitchen Bar serves a range of New York Italian-inspired flatbreads on matchdays plus a range of mezzes that can be enjoyed with a cold beer or cider.

What to drink and where to drink it

- **Nova Scotia**

  Lodged at the tip of Spike Island is an old coaching inn serving farm cider on tap with a view of the marina and the River Avon. Dating back to 1811, it is drenched in history, with pint pots swinging from the bar alongside a large wooden oar presented to the victors of the 1905 London Inter-Hospital Challenge Cup. For the full experience, head to the captain's cabin behind the frosted glass door. The snug is decorated with nautical memorabilia, with a handful of small tables laid out.

- **The Orchard Inn**

  A Mecca for cider lovers, The Orchard Inn is a Victorian boozer with more than 20 ciders and eight cask ales chalked up at any one time. Set in the heart of what was once Bristol's industry hub, it has a working man's charm, with locals' tankards hanging above the bar, a roaring wood burner and walls covered with prints from days of old. You will also find crusty rolls, pies and a plethora of salty snacks on the bar to keep you adequately thirsty.

- **Bristol Beer Factory**

  Tuck into a range of cask, keg and bottled beers at the Bristol Beer Factory, where an assortment of benches, chairs, stools and a rather refined three-piece suite welcome drinkers in a trendy space. To get the whole BBF experience try a wooden paddle filled with three third glasses, which can be filled with your own draught selections.

*With thanks to The Bountyhunter

Bristol Rovers

Introduction

Not all pie brands are born equal, and it was with that in mind that co-founders Jon Simon and Tristan Hogg set about creating Pieminister in 2003 in a bid to revive the reputation of one of Britain's most-loved dishes. Focusing on only the best ingredients and the perfect pastry, they opened their first shop in Stokes Croft, Bristol, hoping their 'moo and blue', 'ruby' and 'free ranger' innovations would take the market by storm. On the first day of trading, they sold five pies, but it wasn't long before the word spread and by 2018 the business was shifting over five million a year and serving up 50 tonnes of mash and 4,500 litres of gravy in its restaurants. The original, just down the road from the Memorial Stadium, still stands today with the brand's slogan graffitied on the wall above. 'Live and eat pie,' it reads, and so we shall.

What to eat and where to eat it

- **The Bristolian**

  Tucked away in historic Picton Street, with outdoor seating sprawling on to the cobblestoned streets, The Bristolian is one of the city's pre-eminent cosmopolitan dining spots, serving one of the best breakfasts around. Veggie, vegan and locally sourced, meaty full English breakfasts can all be found, as well as a 'Bristolian fusion' of chorizo, flatbread, minty yoghurt and eggs.

- **Pieminister, Stokes Croft**

  Visit the home of internationally renowned pie brand Pieminister in Stokes Croft, where you can indulge in one of their classic pie varieties, including the famous 'moo and blue' and 'ruby'. As is common in Bristol, vegetarians and vegans are also well catered for, with a 'mock-a-doodle' tofu 'chicken' pie and the classic 'Heidi'.

- **Oowee**

  Purveyors of deliciously dirty plant-based junk food, Oowee burgers are another Bristolian institution that has successfully transformed the classic meat diner into something a little more sustainable. For anyone who has considered going vegan but thought they couldn't do without their end-of-night kebab, this may just be the place to change your mind.

What to drink and where to drink it

- **The Bell**

  Run by Wrington-based Butcombe Brewery, The Bell pub is one of those pubs you only know about if you know about it. Tucked away on the graffitied Hillgrove Street, you can expect a good selection of real ale, local cider and a jovial atmosphere.

- **The Miner's Arms**

  With purple skirting and a yellow coat of arms, The Miner's Arms is the first pub from award-winning West Country brewers Dawkins. Six real ales are served on tap, including three of Dawkins' own and three guest beers. The Bristol Best is a perfectly agreeable ale to sip on a Saturday afternoon.

- **The Plough Inn**

  Decked to the nines in random pieces of reclaimed oddities, The Plough Inn is an eclectic pub in Easton suburbia, with live music or DJs on most nights. Old amplifiers, record players and instruments hang from the walls inside, but the best is saved for the back, where junkyard booths line the beer garden.

Burnley

> **Fact box**
> Nickname – The Clarets
> Colours – Claret and blue
> Ground – Turf Moor
> Built in – 1883
> Capacity – 21,944

Introduction

Fans accustomed to sipping hot chocolate, Bovril or tea to take the edge off the chill on the terraces might want to brace themselves for something a little different in these parts – Bénédictine. Popular with the locals since the East Lancashire Regiment was stationed in Fécamp, Normandy, during the First World War, it is served with hot water – the Béné & Hot – at Turf Moor, where they go through more than 30 bottles a game. But that pales in comparison to the local Miners' Club, which has its own Bénédictine Lounge in honour of the herbal liqueur. There you will see people of all ages knocking back a Béné, some sipping it hot, some sipping it neat and some who like to keep up with the trends with one of the club's signatures, the Béné Bomb.

What to eat and where to eat it

- **Granada Café**

  Kick off the day in Burnley's historic market hall, which has housed independent traders for more than 700 years. Granted its charter by King Edward I in 1294, tenants have helped preserve the historic atmosphere, with tripe, cow heel, faggots and oatmeal cakes still a common sight. A full English at Granada Café will set you up nicely, with local black pudding a must.

- **Ellis's**

  Tackle the 'straight outta Burnley' burger at Ellis's with a choice of ten varieties of fries to pick from at this humble shack. 'Big mac fries', 'filthy fries' and 'chicken parm fries' sit nicely alongside a good selection of 'pimped' burgers such as the 'gangsta's paradise', 'notorious' and even a peanut butter jelly burger.

- **The Loom Makers Bistro**

  Once the industrial centre of loom making, Burnley was renowned for its mill engines by the late 1880s, when the town was manufacturing more machines than any other place in the country. Today you can visit the world's only surviving operational steam-driven weaving shed at Queen Street Mill or pay homage to its industrial past at this Bank Parade bistro.

What to drink and where to drink it

- **Inn on the Wharf**

  Explore Burnley's historic canal-side and its industrial past in the Weavers' Triangle, which offers a throwback to the days when East Lancashire led the world in the production of cotton cloth. The Inn on the Wharf provides a good vantage point for those who want to get oiled up before the game, both metaphorically and figuratively speaking.

- **The Bridge Bier Huis**

  Enjoy beers from Vocation Brewery, Moorhouse's and Irwell Works at The Bridge Bier Huis, a popular pre-match watering hole offering a vast selection of cask ales, foreign lagers and global bottled beers. A board behind the bar displays the number of different cask ales it has sold since first opening, which is quickly growing into an eye-watering sum.

- **Burnley Miners' Club**

  Visit the world's largest consumer of Bénédictine at the Burnley Miners' Club, where a dedicated lounge pays homage to a liquor brought back from the First World War by local troops stationed in France, who would drink it with hot water to keep them warm. Today the Béné Bomb is a popular choice as a fun alternative to its German equivalent.

Burton Albion

Fact box
Nickname – The Brewers
Colours – Yellow and black
Ground – Pirelli Stadium
Built in – 2005
Capacity – 6,912

Introduction

Brewers Burton Albion is a blessed team indeed, hailing from a town that produces not one but two essential pub staples, Branston Pickle and beer. That is largely down to three things: Spot, snatch and Bass. The origins of brewing in this Staffordshire town can be traced back to the creation of Burton Abbey, when one Wulfric Spot, a Thane of Mercia, gave rise to an ale that would gain national recognition by the late 13th century when the first recorded ditty noted: 'The Abbot of Burton brewed good ale, On Fridays when they fasted, But the Abbot of Burton never tasted his own, As long as his neighbour's lasted.' The beer's quality derives from the town's natural water supply, which has a high presence of sulfate ions from dissolved gypsum in well waters which give off an earthy, eggy smell known in brewing circles as 'Burton snatch'. This distinct flavour became globally renowned several centuries on when Bass ale was exported throughout the British Empire, leading it to become the largest brewery in the world at one point. Today you can enjoy a pint with a pork pie or cheese board in one of the town's famous pubs, served alongside a locally made pickle from Branston.

What to eat and where to eat it

- **The Pickle Pot, Branston**

  Visit the home of the UK's most popular pickle in Branston on the outskirts of Burton upon Trent. There you can pick up a good breakfast panini at The Pickle Pot or a good old cheese and ham baguette with a generous dollop of you know what.

- **Langan's Tea Rooms**

  For those who don't fancy the short excursion to Branston, you will find some excellent, hearty grub at Langan's Tea Rooms in the elegant surroundings of Burton House. Full breakfasts are served, as well as breakfast oatcake wraps (see *Port Vale*). All revenue is ploughed back into community services providing education, training and employment for people who have undergone rehabilitation.

- **The Winery**

  Set in an 11th-century abbey with a riverside terrace, The Winery offers a glimpse of Burton's monastic past, with many of the original features still retained. Enjoy a superb dinner in their company at the end of the day, finishing off with some cheese and pickle.

What to drink and where to drink it

- **The National Brewery Centre**

  Drink and learn at Burton's National Brewery Centre, which incorporates significant elements of the original Bass Collection and displays several fascinating locomotives, vehicles and even shire horses. The Brewery Tap is open to all, serving real ales in the heart of Britain's brewing capital.

- **Beech Hotel**

  There are few better places to enjoy a pre-game pint in Burton than at the Beech Hotel, especially on a warm summer's day when a mobile bar is opened and food is put on. You can find a handful of real ales on tap, but if you want a truly local beer, try out a little-known lager called Carling.

- **Burton Bridge Inn**

  Head to the River Trent to find the brewery tap for one of Burton's oldest independent breweries, the Bridge. Cask ales make the short journey from behind the pub to the bar, including a former Great British Beer Festival winner, the Burton Bridge Bitter. A range of fruit wines are available for those looking for something a little sweeter.

Cambridge United

Fact box
Nickname – The U's
Colours – Amber and black
Ground – Abbey Stadium
Built in – 1923
Capacity – 8,127

Introduction

Of the three thousand or so items listed in *The Foods of England*, just two are linked to the famous university city of Cambridge, an eponymous pudding likened to spotted dick and a sausage. As Lisa Pullen notes in *The Cambridgeshire Cook Book*, 'neither the city nor its storied university, let alone the county writ large, appears to have contributed much of significance to British foodways'. Instead, like its many scholars, the city has been happy to take a learned approach to its gastronomy, allowing outside influences to shape a vibrant and diverse culinary landscape. Within it, you will find butchers, bakers, cheesemongers and micro coffee roasters, brewers, real ale pubs and excellent wine bars. You will discover bhaji Scotch eggs, smoked pork pies and cardamom knots, Portuguese tarts and Sunday lunch sandwiches. In fact, you might say it is one of the best places to eat in the country that has never contributed anything back. Bloody students!

What to eat and where to eat it

- **Bread & Meat**

  Using only British meats alongside homemade mayonnaise and sauces, Bread & Meat is an independent gourmet sandwich shop next to King's College Cambridge. Honey soy chicken, Philly cheesesteak and beef topside can be ordered in a ciabatta, poutine or bowl, but the real star is the porchetta sandwich – pork middle served with fresh salsa verde and crackling.

- **The Cambridge Cheese Company**

  Picture a Cambridge delicatessen and The Cambridge Cheese Company is what you will see. Small, unassuming, packed with charm and with a wicker basket bike propped out front, it is the quintessential university city shop. Pop in for a smoked pork pie, Scotch egg or a hamper of cheese and freshly baked bread.

- **Pint Shop**

  For chargrilled meat dishes and real ales in an old schoolroom setting, head to the Pint Shop, where up to 15 local ales are chalked up in the dining room and an excellent menu of seasonal dishes get swapped in and out. Beef dripping on toast followed by a spit roast shoulder of lamb should give you a flavour, but beware, the menu changes constantly.

What to drink and where to drink it

- **The Cambridge Blue**

  An ideal midway point between train station and stadium, The Cambridge Blue is a superb real ale pub with at least 14 cask ales on at any given time. A dozen keg beers, seven ciders and three fridges filled with hundreds of Belgian beers should also ensure that no one goes thirsty.

- **Live & Let Live**

  Rum and beer lovers will feel at home at this rustic pub next to the Cambridge University Cricket Club. Wooden beams, bar stools, chairs and tables command the room, with beer memorabilia adding to its yesteryear atmosphere.

- **The Cambridge Brew House**

  Take on the craft beer wall at The Cambridge Brew House, a vibrant and modern taproom in the heart of the city centre. Beer flights, good food, relaxed seating and a lively atmosphere await those who prefer something a little more upbeat.

Cardiff City

Fact box
Nickname – The Bluebirds
Colours – Blue
Ground – Cardiff City Stadium
Built in – 2009
Capacity – 33,280

Introduction

In European football, it is pretty rare for a country's principal city to only have one club. Madrid has Real and Atlético, Edinburgh has Hearts and Hibs, Glasgow has Rangers and Celtic. There are 13 professional outfits in London alone, whereas in Turkey, teams from Istanbul make up almost a third of the Süper Lig. Yet Cardiff has only The Bluebirds, which from a gastronomic standpoint allows us to celebrate all that is Welsh on any visit, and all that is Welsh is quite a lot. As street food entrepreneur Simon Thomas says, 'Wales has always been known for being a great place for sourcing ingredients – meat, seafood and dairy produce, in particular'. Dishes such as cawl, Welsh rarebit, laverbread, Welsh cakes, 'bara brith' (literally 'speckled bread') or the Glamorgan sausage have all been regarded as symbols of Welsh food, and places such as Caerphilly, Penderyn and even Snowdonia have given their name to famous delicacies. Most of these can be sampled in Cardiff's bustling markets, cafés, independent eateries and toasty pubs, which do their nation proud on the culinary front. Yaki da to that!

What to eat and where to eat it

- **The Bull Terrier Café**

  Known as the 'Welshman's caviar', laverbread is a luxurious seaweed dish most frequently cultivated on the Pembrokeshire and Carmarthenshire coasts. Have yours as part of a Welsh breakfast special in the Central Market's premier dining establishment, The Bull Terrier Café.

- **Madame Fromage**

  Experience the hearty, homely and warm lamb cawl at the eclectic Madame Fromage in the Castle Quarter Arcades. Succulent lamb pieces are served in a vegetable broth and accompanied by a bap for dipping. Try it with a Black Bomber cheddar from the locally based Snowdonia Cheese Company for starters.

- **The Potted Pig**

  For the best Welsh rarebit in Cardiff head to The Potted Pig, where you can enjoy the cheesy bread alongside a spectacular lamb rump or marinated pork belly. Kick off your dinner with crispy cockles, laverbread butter and focaccia for the whole Cymric experience.

What to drink and where to drink it

- **Cardiff Cottage**

  Find the full Brains range inside the bustling Cardiff Cottage pub on St Mary Street. Built on the footings of a mediaeval burgage plot, it is steeped in history with a narrow frontage and old Victorian tiles decorating the walls. The Brains Brewery clock at the back of the bar will undoubtedly catch your eye, and is surrounded by old ceramic sherry jars.

- **St Canna's Alehouse**

  A short walk from the Cardiff City Stadium, St Canna's Alehouse is a micropub serving local ales from Tiny Rebel, Boss and Tenby Brewers. Beer kegs are loaded up behind the bar and there is plenty of indoor and outdoor seating on their mismatched furniture.

- **Pen & Wig**

  Based in a large converted Victorian terraced house, equidistant between Queen Street and Cathays, the Pen & Wig pub is a popular haunt with several lines of Welsh beer and a friendly atmosphere for after the game. There's outdoor seating at the back and room to mill around at the front too.

Carlisle United

Introduction

There can only be one thing on any weary traveller's mind as they cross the border into Cumbria and thoughts turn to food. Enchantingly long, coiled and subtly seasoned, the Cumberland sausage sits alongside Stilton cheese, Cornish clotted cream and Melton Mowbray pork pies as one of the few British foods to have Protected Geographical Indication (PGI) status. Brought to the region by German miners in the 16th century, it has a distinctly international feel, with exotic spices such as black pepper, nutmeg, marjoram and sage incorporated early thanks to the dynamic port at Whitehaven. To display the PGI mark, the sausages still have to retain these characteristics, being prepared, processed and produced in Cumbria with a meat content of at least 80 per cent. Sausages not meeting these criteria can still be sold as Cumberland sausages but can often have meat content as low as 45 per cent and use emulsified rather than coarse-cut meat, so make sure to look for the PGI badge!

What to eat and where to eat it

- **Crusty Cobbler**

  Get your teeth into a Cumberland sausage within moments of stepping off the train in Carlisle at the Crusty Cobbler café on Botchergate. Sure to satisfy your appetite when paired alongside a portion of chips and gravy.

- **Thin White Duke**

  Tackle a locally sourced Cumberland sausage with mash, crispy onions and onion gravy in a converted monastery building in the heart of Carlisle. The Thin White Duke, a nod to music legend David Bowie, is a trendy eatery and bar offering a diverse range of fresh seasonal dishes and good beers.

- **The Old Bank**

  Treat yourself to a warm black pudding Scotch egg served with Sneck Lifter ale and apple chutney before heading home at The Old Bank in the heart of Carlisle's Historic Quarter. The casual gastropub puts an innovative twist on pub-style dishes with an emphasis on local, seasonal produce.

What to drink and where to drink it

- **The Fat Gadgie**

  An ideal first stop on arrival into Carlisle, The Fat Gadgie is a quirky craft beer venue serving good local ales from Fell Brewery and Carlisle Brewery, among others. Relaxed seating and a chalkboard with space for 16 beers await the weary traveller.

- **The Kings Head**

  It is said that ale has been served on The Kings Head's site since as early as the tenth century, which is not beyond the realms of possibility given its historical look. Exposed brick, wooden beams and well-kept ales can be found in a pub packed with charm.

- **Howard Arms**

  Another historic gem, the Howard Arms has been registered in local directories since 1855, with the exterior Royal Doulton tiles added around 1895. Inside, dimpled leather seats, old board games and Theakstons ales can be found, giving a working museum-like experience.

Charlton Athletic

Fact box
Nickname – The Addicks
Colours – Red
Ground – The Valley
Built in – 1919
Capacity – 27,111

Introduction

Greenwich. The historic home of the Prime Meridian Line, steeped in maritime history and the birthplace of two former monarchs, Henry VIII and Elizabeth I, which for people visiting the south-east borough of London can mean only one thing: you are in for a royal fleecing. Stepping aboard the *Cutty Sark* or taking a look around the Royal Observatory will leave you out of pocket by about £15 each, while you will be lucky to get change out of a £50 note for a couple of rounds of fish and chips and two pints at The Gipsy Moth. In fact, stay around the historic old town and you are guaranteed not to find a cup of tea for under £3 or a decent pint for under £6. The air is free, but if you want to travel through it on the Peninsula cable car, that will set you back £3.50 each way. Alternatively, step off the train at Deptford, or Westcombe Park, or even, if you search really hard, Charlton, and you will find a bevy of eating and drinking spots, all out of reach of the day trippers and the tourist tax they bring with them.

What to eat and where to eat it

- **Valley Café**

  Perhaps one of the best and certainly one of the most south-east London places to eat in Charlton, the Valley Café serves up honest grub at a fair price in a no-nonsense setting. A breakfast of sausage, bacon, bubble and eggs is a fine way to kick off the day, washed down with a mug of builder's tea.

- **Goddards at Greenwich**

  Traditional pie and mash shops are becoming a rare breed in this part of the country, which is a great shame. But one you can foresee being around for a while is Goddards at Greenwich, which, as well as knocking out a tremendous minced beef and liquor, also supplies increasingly popular chicken and ham, and lamb and rosemary fillings.

- **Sparrow**

  Escape the hustle and bustle of The Valley and the packed train out of Charlton by making a stop off at Sparrow restaurant in Lewisham, less than a ten-minute journey from the ground. Small plates of seasonal dishes are chalked up and soon fill the table in the contemporary, chic setting.

What to drink and where to drink it

- **Villages**
Not included in the Bermondsey Beer Mile (see *Millwall*) but very much in keeping with its vibe, Villages is a microbrewery and taproom under the arches in Deptford. Rodeo and Rafiki are popular choices. They also have an unfiltered lager, Whistle, if you prefer something with fewer hops.

- **Taproom SE8**
Fine house microbrews and pizza presented in a funky, warehouse-like setting at Taproom SE8 in the newly renovated marketplace outside Deptford station. A cinema-style letter board behind the bar displays the beers, most of which are brewed within five miles of the bar.

- **The River Ale House**
Alight at Westcombe Park for The River Ale House, a wooden-clad micropub where real ales, real cider and Belgian beers are in good supply. Kentish brews get a good showing here, with The Canterbury Ales, Goody Ales and Kent Brewery regular fixtures.

Chelsea

Fact box
Nickname – The Blues
Colours – Blue
Ground – Stamford Bridge
Built in – 1876
Capacity – 41,837

Introduction

Chelsea FC's loyal supporters have become well acquainted with sell-out crowds at Stamford Bridge ever since they welcomed a Russian oligarch to the club and started, you know, winning things. But long before The Blues had any money, a stadium, or even a game to play, some 50,000 people are reported to have turned up to the London borough one Good Friday in search of something else – the Chelsea bun. Sticky, sweet, filled with raisins and topped with a sugary glaze, the sweet treat caused quite a stir when it was first created at the Old Chelsea Bun House in the 16th century, so much so that the bakers had to sell them through openings in the shutters and a strong police presence was needed to keep the order. As one local poet wrote at the time, they were as 'fragrant as honey and sweeter in taste' and 'as flaky and white as if baked by the light', while Lewis Carroll paid tribute to them in one of his short stories, *A Tangled Tale*, in 1880 when one of the characters says: 'Give her a Chelsea bun, miss! That's what most young ladies like best.' The Old Bun House no longer exists today, replaced by a textiles and furniture shop run by people who are 'preoccupied', nay, 'obsessed' with the way things are made. It is an apt transformation of an area that has become all glaze and no bun.

What to eat and where to eat it

- **The Veterans Kitchen**

  Founded in a bid to help veterans who had fallen on bad times to recover, The Veterans Kitchen continues to be staffed by people who have served in the HM Armed Forces. They serve up a cracking pre-match breakfast. Get the complete works with a pot of tea for a very reasonable price for these parts.

- **Megan's**

  Finding a good Chelsea bun in Chelsea is easier said than done these days, but thankfully Megan's usually has them in good supply, along with several other delicious breakfast, brunch and lunch options.

- **The Troubadour**

  For good food, good music and good times, head over to The Troubadour post-match, where you will find fantastic British cuisine above a historic live music venue. Extensive collections of oddities line the walls and ceilings, with diners huddled together to create a warming, communal atmosphere.

What to drink and where to drink it

- **The Harwood Arms**

  Forget everything you think you know about the Scotch egg, because you haven't tried one until you sink your teeth into the crispy crust of The Harwood Arms' venison variation and experienced the textural delight that meets your lips before they plunge into the runny egg in the middle. Enjoy with a nice jar of ale.

- **Cock Tavern**

  Head to the Cock Tavern for a pint and a pork pie before the game, where you will find plenty of local London brews to try out. Gipsy Hill, Brixton and Partizan are among those usually on tap, with a lovely big beer garden to enjoy them in if the sun is out.

- **The White Horse**

  Take the tube south after the game if you want to avoid big crowds getting back into the city. At Parsons Green, you will find The White Horse, which can be relied upon for having a good selection of ales on tap, including local craft beers.

Cheltenham Town

Introduction

If you want to get a feel for how passionate the people of Gloucestershire are about their cheeses, stand atop Cooper's Hill and ask yourself, would I throw myself down this? If the answer is no then good, you are one of the sane ones. If it is yes, then you might want to consider the annual championships, which sees locals toss themselves down the valley in pursuit of a wheel of double Gloucestershire cheese. The winner is awarded with a delicacy that has been made in these parts since the 16th century using milk from local cows, which were almost extinct until recently when Charles Martell was offered a blank cheque by British cheese saviour Patrick Rance and went about reviving the breed. The dairy takes the cream from one night's milking and also the following day's milking, hence the 'double'. Along with its 'single' sister – the Diet Coke version – it joins several other famed cheese varieties made in these parts, such as May Hill Green, Cerney Pyramid and Cotswold. But one that will test your nerves in a slightly different way is the Stinking Bishop of Dymock, which gets its honking smell from being immersed in perry made from the local Stinking Bishop pear, from which the name is derived. If you can bear the scent, the creamy flavours that follow are well worth the punt.

What to eat and where to eat it

- **WoodKraft Cheltenham**

  Get acquainted with Gloucestershire's native pig at the WoodKraft café, which lies midway between Cheltenham Spa and Jonny-Rocks Stadium. Gloucester Old Spot sausages and Old Spot streaky bacon are included in the full English at the trendy artisanal café.

- **The Cheeseworks**

  Pack a picnic of some of the best cheeses, chutneys, ales and ciders in the land at The Cheeseworks. A blue log and brie from the Cotswolds, single and double Gloucester and Stinking Bishop line the walls ready to be sampled, hand-cut and wrapped in wax paper.

- **Domaine 16**

  There is no shortage of cheese at Domaine 16, where you can get your fix as part of a sharing board, fondue or as a tasty starter dish. Enjoy it with a nice glass of Cotswold Classic sparkling wine from Woodchester Valley or a Poulton Hill Estate Bacchus.

What to drink and where to drink it

- **DEYA Brewing Company**

  Step off the train and into one of Britain's most popular craft brewers at the DEYA taproom and brewery. Find their punchy pale ale, Steady Rolling Man, on tap, as well as the full range of beers in the fridge. On sunny days benches are arranged outside, with food stalls often running.

- **Sandford Park Alehouse**

  Rows of cask and keg ales line the bar at the Sandford Park Alehouse, with several local ciders available to sample too. Beers from Cheltenham's DEYA usually make an appearance along with Warwickshire's Purity Brewing, Herefordshire's Wye Valley and Devonshire cider.

- **Jolly Brewmaster**

  One of the much-loved smaller pubs of Cheltenham, the Jolly Brewmaster showcases all the hallmarks of an excellent real ale pub with a log fire, hot pies, cheese selections and a great range of beers. There is also a generously sized beer garden for hot days.

Colchester United

Fact box
Nickname – The U's
Colours – Blue and white
Ground – Colchester Community Stadium
Built in – 2007
Capacity – 10,105

Introduction

Every year on the first Friday of September, a flotilla of boats heads out into the Colne estuary off Mersea Island, just south of Colchester, to take part in the time-honoured Opening of the Oyster Fishery. The town's mayor, chief executive and town sergeant sail aboard a dredger in full regalia to read the proclamation of 1256 and eat the first oyster of the season, before making a gin and gingerbread toast to the Queen per the ancient custom. Shortly after this, in October, hundreds of invited guests and dignitaries gather at the Town Hall for an oyster feast, which has been held in some form since at least 1318 when oystermen, pockets full of harvest money, would descend on the High Street to indulge in traditional feasting and drinking in what is known as Colchester's own Oktoberfest. It also became popular with London folk, which was a big step in transforming oysters from a 'poor man's' food into a delicacy. By the late 19th century, a host of VIPs from the capital, including the Lord Mayor, would travel by special train to attend the event, consuming some 12,000 of the 'Colchester natives' alongside the local townspeople over the day.

What to eat and where to eat it

- **Timbers**

  Shiver me timbers. If this isn't one of the best breakfast places in the whole of Essex then I don't know what is. Housed in a historic sticky-outy building on Trinity Street, the sprawling big breakfast uses fresh meat from Proctors Butchers as part of an ensemble that is sure to set you up for the day.

- **GreyFriars Hotel**

  One of the best and (regrettably) only places to serve Colchester natives and Mersea rock oysters in the town, the GreyFriars Hotel includes both (depending on the season) as part of its à la carte menu alongside lemon, shallot vinegar and Tabasco.

- **The Old Siege House Bar & Brasserie**

  Named after the siege of Colchester that dates back to the English Civil War era, The Old Siege House Bar & Brasserie is a historic dining space located next to the River Colne. Classically cooked dishes are served in an ambient setting. You might even spot remains from the siege, with the west side's timber frames and south front of the building still containing bullet holes.

What to drink and where to drink it

- **The Ale House**

  Find ales from Colchester Brewery alongside Harwich Town Brewing, Witham and Maldon at The Ale House near Colchester Town (not to be confused with Colchester North) train station. The old detached building has a comforting, if slightly dated, vibe, which is no bad thing.

- **Queen St Brewhouse**

  Head to the bottom of the High Street to discover one of Colchester's more quirky-looking pubs, with a rough and ready exterior making way for a cosy but surprisingly spacious inside. Comfortable bar stools and reclaimed chairs and tables fill the ground floor, with a small room available upstairs.

- **Three Wise Monkeys**

  Partake in Colchester's time-honoured tradition of making a gin toast to the Queen at the Three Wise Monkeys bar in the centre of town. An entire basement is dedicated to the popular spirit, with several ginger versions available for those who want the full proclamation experience.

Coventry City

Fact box
Nickname – The Sky Blues
Colours – Sky blue
Ground – Ricoh Arena
Built in – 2005
Capacity – 32,753

Introduction

Traditional Midlands cuisine has a fight for survival on its hands. That was the conclusion of a new poll released by *Love British Food Fortnight*, which corresponded with a similar study (see *Aston Villa*) warning that many Black Country dishes could be wiped out within the next 50 years. Chief among the dishes destined for the dustbin was the 'Coventry Godcake', with only two per cent of respondents claiming to have ever heard of it. The triangular pastry akin to a mince pie or Eccles cake was conventionally presented by godparents to their godchildren (hence the name) along with a blessing for the year ahead. But as the tradition fell into decline, so did the delicacy, and before long it had disappeared from café countertops in Coventry. Thankfully, like Mr Grorty Dick of the faggot revival (see *Walsall*), there were local heroes at the ready to revive the iconic pastry, with baker Leigh Waite leading the 'holy charge' and getting it back on the menu at Esquires in the city's Transport Museum, and songwriter David Goody, whose previous hits include 'Rules of the Coventry Ring Road', penning an ode to the triangular Sky Blue snack. As he melodically argues, it is high time to forget our trendy obsession with cupcakes, 'it is the English classics that we must partake'. Amen to that.

What to eat and where to eat it

- **Playwrights**

  An independently owned bistro in the heart of Coventry's Cathedral Quarter, Playwrights prides itself on providing delicious food cooked with fresh produce from local suppliers. On dry days tables are lined up along the cobblestoned streets, with an excellent breakfast to be had if you arrive early enough.

- **Esquires, Coventry Transport Museum**

  One of the few remaining places in the country where you are likely to find Coventry Godcakes, Esquires of the Transport Museum makes for an ideal rest stop on the site of one of the largest British road transport collections in the world.

- **The Green Dragon**

  Housed in a mediaeval building constructed in 1450 and named The Green Dragon Inn since 1500, this historic dining spot takes its place in the community seriously, using local produce and supporting independent suppliers. Menus are rotated with the seasons, and you will find a good selection of local drinks to try too.

What to drink and where to drink it

- **Twisted Barrel Tap House**

  Enjoy the Twisted Barrel core range while standing next to the very tanks they are brewed in at the Tap House next to Sky Blue Way. A session IPA, Triple Berry Sour and Peanut Butter Imperial Stout are among the regulars in this hip drinking spot.

- **Broomfield Tavern**

  A Victorian pub that has remained largely untouched over time, the Broomfield Tavern is the sort of place that makes you immediately think, 'yes, this is where I belong'. Serving real ales and ciders in a warm, traditional pub setting, it is the perfect place to pass a few hours before the game.

- **Castle Yard Tap Room**

  Yes, Coventry has a castle, and yes, there is a fantastic taproom in the old grounds serving some delightful local ales and lagers. It has its own courtyard where, on sunny days, you can catch some rays out in its historic surroundings.

Crawley Town

Fact box
Nickname – The Reds
Colours – Red
Ground – Broadfield Stadium
Built in – 1997
Capacity – 6,134

Introduction

When the New Towns Act was passed in 1946 to deal with urban congestion and housing shortages, the Reith Commission decreed that the make-up of Britain's new dwellings should revolve around three things: primary and nursery schools, a shop selling staple foods and, most importantly, a pub. For Crawley, which joined Stevenage, Basildon and Bracknell in the first generation of developments to create a ring around London, there already existed much of what made towns work, having been close to industry for most of its history. By April 1960, when the town's population had reached 51,700, only 70 people were registered as unemployed. Shortly after, the 11th neighbourhood, Broadfield, was developed along with Broadfield Stadium, home to Crawley Town from 1997. The stadium backs on to two schools, shops and, (stated above) The New Moon pub.

What to eat and where to eat it

- **Sage Vegan Café**

  Get your day off to a healthy and wholesome start at Sage Vegan Café, where a 'full vegland' breakfast and 'super energiser' smoothie go down a treat. If you get there a bit later, the 'grilled kofte kebab' served on flatbread with chilli sauce, olives, raita and chips is a real treat. That or the 'aubergine peanut butter curry'.

- **Fatboys Joint Afghan Canteen**

  It's not every day you get to sample an Afghan artisan smashed burger, but thanks to Fatboy and his native joint you can take your pick of ten of them, ranging from the 'cheeky chapli' to the 'smoking snakebite'. Wash down with a mint lemonade – it does wonders for digestion.

- **Taj the Grocer**

  The best place to collect post-match snacks for the journey home, Taj the Grocer is a gem of a supermarket located within the main shopping precinct in Crawley town centre. A vast array of fresh produce is displayed at the shop's front, offering exotic fruits such as dates, prunes and figs for those interested. But the best stuff is found behind the counter, where delightful vegetable and lamb samosas are kept warm.

What to drink and where to drink it

- **Railway**

  With a perfect CAMRA beer cellar rating and idyllic location between the train station and the stadium, Railway is an excellent place to make a pit stop right next to the Brighton main line and Crawley's historic signal box. Drink Sussex Best from Harvey's Brewery for a taste of the local stuff.

- **The New Moon**

  A popular haunt with fans before the game, The New Moon is a traditional pub within a short walk of Broadfield Stadium. Formerly the Half Moon Inn, it dates back to the 19th century when it served as a rest stop for weary travellers on the long Brighton Road.

- **The Old Punch Bowl**

  Crawley may be known as a new town, but parts of it are, in fact, quite historic. Hidden behind its modern shopping precincts lies an old High Street that dates back several centuries. The Old Punch Bowl is a mediaeval timber-framed Wealden hall house that has been wonderfully preserved and is the perfect spot to relax after the game.

Crewe Alexandra

Fact box
Nickname – The Railwaymen
Colours – Red
Ground – Gresty Road
Built in – 1906
Capacity – 10,153

Introduction

In the late 1920s, Florence White set out on a mission to put down in writing all of the traditional English recipes that she felt were in danger of being lost. Using recipes passed down through generations, scribbled on scraps of paper or included in some of the earliest cookbooks, she created a compendium of regional recipes that stretched from the Eccles cake of Lancashire (see *Salford City*) to the Godcake of Coventry (see *Coventry City*) and the junket of Devonshire. But it is perhaps surprising that, when it comes to one of the country's most celebrated savoury treats, the pork pie, the recipe for the Cheshire variant predates that of the Melton Mowbray. Wedged between a 'Rough Puff Pastry' and a 'Chitterling Turnover', White takes a recipe penned by Hannah Glasse in 1747 in the bestselling book *The Art of Cookery*, which calls for pork loin, a good crust and half a pint of white wine to make the pie (a pint if 'your pie be large'). The entrant for its Leicestershire equivalent is relatively modern in comparison, although given its acclaim one can only assume it is either better or more economical. Either way, who would have known!

What to eat and where to eat it

- **Finigan's Bakery**

  There's only one way to start the day in the railway town of Crewe, and that is with a bacon, sausage and egg 'doorstep' sandwich next to the wagon works on Gresty Road. Finigan's has been serving the local community for 34 years with its freshly baked bread, pies and cakes, baked in one of the oldest commercial brick-bottom ovens in the area.

- **Benny's Fish and Chips**

  One of the Football League's iconic stadium chippies, Benny's is snugly tucked into a row of terraced housing a stone's throw from Gresty Road's Main Stand. A bargain tray of fish strips, chips, sausage and mushy peas is a touch before the game, especially if you are up on a cold Tuesday night.

- **Chatwins**

  Get your pork pie haul at Chatwins in the Victoria Centre, baked through the night in nearby Nantwich. It also sells superb pork and apple pastries as well as oval steak pies with tasty chunks of meat and thick gravy.

What to drink and where to drink it

- **Hops Belgian Style Café Bar**

  For travelling football fans Hops Belgian Style Café Bar should come with a disclaimer: it's easy to find but impossibly hard to leave when kick-off time approaches. Based in an old red-bricked house with a charming beer garden, you will find a host of real ales, Belgian beer and charcuterie in one of the north-west's finest boozers.

- **The Borough Arms**

  Set next to the West Coast Main Line, The Borough Arms real ale house is the very definition of 'proper', with a warm pub feel and the smell of a busy cellar emanating from below the decks. Housing up to ten cask beers at any one point, all beers are chalked up above the bar ready for consumption.

- **Tom's Tap and Brewhouse**

  A promising upstart, Tom's Tap and Brewhouse is a small-scale brewery on Crewe's outskirts just down the road from The Borough Arms. On sunny days you can sit outside and watch the trains whiz past as you indulge in a good range of freshly made beer.

Crystal Palace

Introduction

Had this book been published in 1851, it could have been quite popular among the Crystal Palace exhibition attendees, many of whom were quick to bemoan on-site catering efforts in a series of letters published in *The Morning Chronicle*. One described the food on offer as the 'worst and smallest sandwiches I have ever tasted', while others picked fault at the 'little, dry, sixpenny dollops of pork pie'. Schweppes, which won the government contract, supplied over two million Bath buns, 1.1 million bottles of carbonated water and 1,000 gallons of pickles via a central tea room during the event, which was put on to showcase the merits of internationalism. Today south London is awash with global cuisines which would put the traditional British fare on offer to shame. But it is still worth taking a short walk to find the best of the bunch.

What to eat and where to eat it

- **Joanna's**

  Kick off the day with 'the English' at Joanna's, where you'll find old-fashioned wood panelling, wooden furnishings and broadsheet newspapers draped over wall racks ready for your perusal. Eggs, bacon and sausage are served alongside a roast tomato and mushroom sautéed potato. Mushrooms on toast with chive cream cheese is also a fair shout, as is the smoked salmon and cream cheese bagel.

- **Morley's Chicken**

  A south London institution, Morley's Chicken is widely tipped to be superior to its Kentucky rival by those who frequent it. Serving up its own secret combination of herbs and spices, it won acclaim in 2017 when it appeared on the Chicken Connoisseur's famed YouTube series *The Pengest Munch*. The classic meal – burger, chips and drink – was proclaimed 'delicious', while the added wings 'banged'. Definitely one for the bucket list.

- **Roti Brothers**

  A former food truck with permanent lodgings in SE19, this burger joint will put any stadium equivalent to shame. The marinated buttermilk buffalo chicken burger is a favourite among locals who swarm to its humble premises, marked by graffiti on the walls. A chicken chilli pesto burger and 'Bro's Philly Wrap' are also popular, served with rosemary chips, spiced garlic mayo and creamy chimichurri.

What to drink and where to drink it

- **The Gipsy Hill Taproom**

  Founded in 2014 following a confab in The Rake in Borough Market (well worth a visit if you head out via London Bridge) between two beer enthusiasts, Gipsy Hill has grown into a formidable outfit based around principles of quality, innovation and community. You'll get plenty of the latter in their taproom, which has a warm industrial feel to it and a wide range of craft beers to choose from.

- **Claret & Ale**

  Discover the famous beer board at the Claret & Ale in Addiscombe. Wedged between a row of retail units, the friendly pub offers a superb range of real ales which get chalked up on a patchwork of tiles before being shuffled into position like a game of Rummikub. The rotating beer selection has won it several accolades, including CAMRA borough Pub of the Year for Croydon on numerous occasions.

- **The Oval Tavern**

  Hidden down a quiet residential street sits a 'true oasis of a pub' known for its cosy, community atmosphere and an excellent selection of local brews. The Cronx Brewery, based just down the road, gets a good showing in here, offering 'great beer straight outta Croydon'. A wide array of musical acts takes to the stage at night, making it an ideal place to finish the day.

Derby County

Fact box
Nickname – The Rams
Colours – White
Ground – Pride Park
Built in – 1997
Capacity – 33,597

Introduction

Few people can claim to have had as significant an impact on America's baseball stadiums as Derby-born Harry M. Stevens. Not only did he create the scorecard used by spectators to this day, he also came up with the idea of selling bottles of fizzy drinks with straws so that fans didn't miss an important play while taking a swig from the bottle. But his most significant contribution to the ballpark experience was made on a chilly April day in 1901 after he ordered his staff to stuff 'dachshund sausages' (brought to the States by German immigrants) into bread rolls. A *New York Journal* sports cartoonist, quite taken aback by this new culinary creation, sketched one vendor making his way through the stands as he shouted, 'They're red hot! Get your dachshund sausages while they're red hot!' But unsure how to spell dachshund he simply wrote 'hot dog' instead, and the trend caught on. Today hundreds of millions of hot dogs are sold at ball grounds, many of which have been adapted by the clubs. The 'Fenway Frank' of Boston is among the most popular, but the Atlanta Braves's 'T.E.D.' (The Everything Dog) and San

Francisco Giants's 'Sheboygan Sausage' are also worthy incarnations of the first-ever 'Derby Dog' to have graced their stadiums.

What to eat and where to eat it

- **Derby Pyclet Parlour**

  Somewhere between an oatcake (see *Port Vale*), a pancake and a crumpet, the pyclet is a Derbyshire special that has made its way back on to the menu thanks to the Pyclet Parlour. Using the same recipe as devised by the monks in 1864, this is the perfect place to kick off the day with a traditional breakfast pyclet or a 'posh pyclet' made with smoked salmon, Stilton or goat's cheese.

- **Bunk**

  Doff your cap to a Derbyshire legend who transformed the stateside ballpark experience at Bunk, a retro eatery on Sadler Gate. Kick off with a basket of wings before tucking into a dachshund in bread, with unlimited toppings available.

- **Bustler Market**

  A street food venue in the heart of Derby's industrial quarter, Bustler Market is an ideal place to get a taste of the city, with an impressive array of stalls supplying everything from chilli cheese fries to hoppy craft beer. A 'fat snags' hot dog served in a sourdough and buttermilk bun is a must if you can find one.

What to drink and where to drink it

- **The Tap**

  Settle in at this warm, cosy, country-chic taproom for the full range of Derby Brewing Company beers. You will typically find at least half a dozen ales from the local brewers next to guest ales from elsewhere, which get chalked up by the bar.

- **Suds & Soda**

  Home to the largest selection of beers in Derby, taproom and bottle bar Suds & Soda boasts a bountiful collection of local, national and global craft beers. Discover brews from Nottingham's Neon Raptor and Liquid Light, Birmingham's GlassHouse and even a Midland's cider from Hogan's.

- **The Exeter Arms**

  Finish the day with a smooth pint of real ale and splendid cheese board at The Exeter Arms, bringing rural charm into the heart of the city. Home to the Dancing Duck Brewery, you will discover their superb core range along with a few seasonal specials that include a 'no-nonsense brown ale' called Brian Clough, and a Beaky Blinder.

Doncaster Rovers

Fact box
Nickname – The Vikings
Colours – Red and white
Ground – Keepmoat Stadium
Built in – 2006
Capacity – 15,231

Introduction

A club's nickname is often a good place to start if you want to get a feel for the place it represents, but it is surprising how few fall under the food and beverage banner. Indeed, of the 92 clubs competing on the Football League pyramid, only Burton Albion (The Brewers) and Reading (The Biscuitmen) feature, with a few others loosely flirting with it. Had Doncaster Rovers chosen to adopt the Butterscotchmen in a nod to the confectionery treat that hails from the area they could have bolstered the list. Parkinson's of Doncaster is credited with the invention of butterscotch boiled sweets in 1817, selling them in tins which became one of the town's best-known exports. They became famous in 1851 when Queen Victoria was presented with a tin when she visited the South Yorkshire city.

What to eat and where to eat it

- **Clam & Cork**

  Doncaster may be among the most landlocked places in Britain, but it would be sinful not to experience this small seafood café in the heart of its fish market. Occupying a former wet fish stand, it has a freshness guaranteed stamp, with a catch that arrives daily. Sample crab claws in tempura batter with a garlic and lime mayo dip, scallops with slivers of crackling or a south Indian fish curry if you want something more substantial.

- **Wool Market**

  Like most places, Doncaster has been blessed with a magnificent food hall where you will be spoilt for choice among the many stands that occupy the historic commercial building in the heart of the town. Grab an excellent breakfast butty at The Barnyard or sample a kathi roll in the Indian Street Food Hawker. You can even check out the mediaeval well discovered during the works and now preserved under a glass floor.

- **The City Doncaster**

  An innovative and inviting menu awaits you at The City Doncaster, where diners can tuck into a strong sampling of European dishes that underpin the town's multicultural vibrancy. Cabbage stew, grilled smoked cheese from Poland and a sour rye soup that hails from West Slavic countries are on offer as an entrée, while classic goulash, schnitzel and duck breast with Bison Grass vodka sauce form a robust main course menu.

What to drink and where to drink it

- ### The Draughtsman Alehouse

Doncaster has a proud railway heritage. The first locomotive works were established in the heart of the town centre in 1853 by the Great Northern Railway, transforming Doncaster from a peaceful Georgian market town into an engineering superpower. Today you can raise a jar to its pioneering forebears at The Draughtsman Alehouse, as high-speed trains from all corners of the country pass by. A snug and cosy setting that makes a worthy first port of call.

- ### Doncaster Brewery

Take a journey through Doncaster's history at its namesake brewery, which celebrates the town's heritage in a bid to put it back on the map. Kick off the day with a Mansion House mild, which pays homage to one of only three such buildings in the UK. A Muck Bucket IPA remembers Doncaster's coal and railway legacy, while the Charter porter is named after the Charter granted by King Richard I on 2 May 1194, which gave Doncaster national recognition as a town.

- ### The Salutation

Other than trains and butterscotch, Doncaster is probably best known for one thing: horse racing. The St Ledger was first held in 1776 and the Doncaster Cup is the oldest continuing regulated horse race in the world. South Parade connects the town to the racecourse and, handily, the Keepmoat Stadium. On it stands The Salutation, which reflects the prosperity brought about by its fashionable status as a racing town.

Everton

Fact box
Nickname – The Toffees
Colours – Blue
Ground – Goodison Park
Built in – 1892
Capacity – 39,414

Introduction

A taste of Liverpool is best experienced when viewed through two lenses, one primed on local cuisines and the other on gastronomy that has been brought to the city from afar. As the elder of two clubs, Everton, which occupied Anfield until the club was booted out in 1892, is perhaps best placed to become acquainted with the former, particularly given the link to the popular boiled 'Everton Mint' sweet, which was first produced in a sweet shop outside the club's second home, Goodison Park. The shop's owner, Mother Noblett, created the mints to appeal to Everton fans, making them black and white in honour of the team's then black-and-white kit. She even persuaded the club to let a girl walk around the ground before matches, throwing mints into the crowd. They remain popular to this day, even though Everton have since changed their kit colour to blue.

What to eat and where to eat it

- **Café Tabac**

  A Bold Street institution, Café Tabac has been on Liverpool's bohemian café/bar scene for over 40 years. Popular with actors, singers and performers, Holly Johnson, the former lead vocalist of Frankie Goes to Hollywood, once reminisced that if he ever had money for food when he was young it was 'always spent on a sausage and apple sauce sandwich at Tabac'. Today its 'builder's breakfast' is renowned, usually among those with big appetites – or bad hangovers.

- **Baltic Fleet**

  If you ever wondered about the origin of the word 'Scouser', head down to the Baltic Fleet and order yourself a stew that is widely known around northern European seaports but less so elsewhere. Scouse, derived from lobscouse, is a hearty mash of meat, veg and gravy that will leave you well prepared to battle the coastal elements. Best enjoyed on the docks with crusty bread and beetroot on the side.

- **Fodder Canteen**

  Home of the 'Scouse afternoon tea' and purveyors of the famous local cake 'Wet Nelly', Fodder Canteen is a no-nonsense tribute to the many home-cooked favourites that call Liverpool home. Enjoy 'peawack soup' or the Fodder's own take on high tea in its quirky Baltic space, a three-tiered wonder that includes 'Scouse balls', 'peawack puffs', 'Liverpool Judy', 'Wet Nelly' and jam butties from Knotty Ash.

THE GREAT PIE REVOLT

What to drink and where to drink it

- **The Ship & Mitre**

  With the largest selection of hand-pulled ales on Merseyside and one of the largest selections of bottled beers in the north-west, The Ship & Mitre, located in the heart of the city, is easy to find but hard to leave for any ale enthusiast. Its own brewery also offers small-batch brews with a freshness guarantee of grain to glass in less than a month. You will find a good selection on the bar on most days.

- **Love Lane Brewery**

  Set in the heart of the 'coolest district in the UK', Love Lane Brewery lives up to its surroundings with a modern, chic taproom housed in an old rubber factory. Alongside a wide range of regular and limited-edition ales, they are also custodians of the historic Higson's brand and home to Ginsmiths of Liverpool Distillery where Merchant Navy, Dry and an award-winning Marshmallow gin are produced.

- **Lady of Mann**

  Named after the eponymous Manx ferry, the smartly dressed Lady of Mann is located on Liverpool's Dale Street in the historic Thomas Rigby's buildings, a stone's throw from the Cavern Club and the Beatles museum. You'll find local gins and Isle of Mann beers in a cosy setting that is ideal for kicking back after the match.

Exeter City

Fact box
Nickname – The Grecians
Colours – Red and white
Ground – St James Park
Built in – 1904
Capacity – 8,696

Introduction

Debates over how to assemble a scone are as heated as they get in this part of the country. While those in Devon typically spread the clotted cream first, followed by jam (the 'Devonian way'), the 'Cornish method' is to spread the jam first, followed by the cream. In 2018 there was an outcry after a National Trust property published a cream tea advert featuring a scone with the cream on before the jam, resulting in the Queen's own chef having to step in to settle the matter himself (he voted Cornish). But the feud doesn't end there. Having started as a cottage industry made up of local farms and dairies, clotted cream was soon industrialised as tea rooms in London, Harrogate (see *Harrogate Town*) and Bath fuelled demand for the high tea staple. One manufacturer, Definitely Devon, succumbed to capitalist forces and in 2011 sold out to Rodda's, who moved production to Cornwall, prompting an investigation by Trading Standards. What's more, a certain Frances Rodda was the man responsible for setting up commercial links in London and likely convincing them, and consequently the Queen, to spread the cream on top of the jam as per the Cornish custom. A double kick in the udders for Devon!

What to eat and where to eat it

- **Brody's Breakfast Bistro**
For a breakfast of champions, make your first stop Brody's Breakfast Bistro and get stuck into its innovative buffet-style dining experience. Unlimited food and drink await the weary traveller, so just grab a plate and help yourself.

- **Tea on the Green**
Take in views of the cathedral as you lather lashings of clotted cream on your scone *before* the jam at Tea on the Green. The restaurant is based in a 16th-century building and has a good breakfast and lunch menu too.

- **Rockfish**
With the bounty of Brixham harbour on their doorstep, Rockfish serves up fresh catches brought in daily from its own boat, the *Rockfisher*, and marked down on your tablecloth. From sea to plate within hours, this is one of the freshest seafood experiences in Devon.

What to drink and where to drink it

- **The Beer Cellar**

  A beer emporium housed in a small, blink-and-you'll-miss-it-sized bar next to the cathedral, The Beer Cellar regularly has more than ten ales and ciders on draught and a good selection of bottles in the fridge. Penpont Brewery and The Rebel Brewing Co. are regular features.

- **Samuel Jones**

  Smoke and alehouse Samuel Jones is the perfect place to unwind next to the quay. Retaining its industrial heritage, the trendy bar has beer from St Austell, Beerd and some good ciders.

- **The Sample Room**

  Set in the arches beneath Exeter St Thomas railway station, The Sample Room is a boutique bar serving a house range of gins, vodkas and absinthes, among other things. The perfect place to hide out in the event of a gritty win or a humbling defeat, it makes for a quirky and fun end to the day.

Fleetwood Town

Fact box
Nickname – The Fishermen
Colours – Red and white
Ground – Highbury Stadium
Built in – 1939
Capacity – 5,327

Introduction

The Fishermen of Fleetwood have a nautical heritage that spans back to the late 19th century when fleets of fishing smacks – wind-powered boats evolved specifically for work in the tricky waters of the Irish Sea and north-west coast – built up the town's reputation for hake catches. Until then – and to a large extent still now – hake wasn't a popular fish, but it allowed Fleetwood to grow into one of Britain's eminent fishing ports. Today one of the boats, named *Harriet*, is on show in Fleetwood's oldest building, which serves as a museum. Its prized catch can also still be sampled in one of the many fish bars, where a drive for more sustainable fish has seen it gain popularity once again.

What to eat and where to eat it

- ### The Eating House

  At the end of the alley you'll find Carol and Jason's The Eating House serving up proper grub in an unpretentious setting just moments away from Fleetwood Market, Pharos Lighthouse and the harbour front. If you get there early, the full English breakfast will put you in good form for the rest of the day, although a healthy portion of liver and onions with a mug of milky coffee will equally do the trick.

- ### Granada Fish Bar

  Established in 1890 in the heyday of Fleetwood's fishing industry, Granada Fish Bar is a multi-award-winning fish and chip shop in the heart of town. Take a pick of cod, haddock, plaice, lemon sole and, of course, hake, just moments away from the old *Harriet* fishing smack, with the mouth of the Wyre also nearby if you fancy eating al fresco on the seafront.

- ### The Trafalgar

  Finish off the day in one of Lancashire's leading seafood restaurants, where a family team pay homage to the Fylde Coast and Fleetwood's fishing heritage with a good range of dishes that rotate with the seasons and the best catch. Try the 'famous fish soup' as an entrée before consulting the blackboard where the best selections are chalked up daily, with hake a regular feature along with halibut and haddock.

What to drink and where to drink it

- **Royal Oak Pub, aka 'Dead'uns'**

  Celebrate Fleetwood's proud maritime history in the Royal Oak Pub, which serves a large selection of perfectly conditioned local ales in a cosy pub setting. Its alternative moniker, Dead'uns, is rumoured to originate from a former landlord who would keep a paternal eye over the local fishermen. If he thought they had had one too many he would refuse their pint pot by saying, 'this one's a dead 'un, go home to your wife'.

- **The Strawberry Gardens Pub**

  Immerse yourself in the beer wall of fame at The Strawberry Gardens Pub, which occupies an old hotel a short walk away from Highbury Stadium. Eighteen handpumps serve various local real ales and cask ciders, with Skippool Creek one to look out for, from a nano brewery based in Thornton-Cleveleys on the Fylde Coast.

- **Steamer**

  Find ales from across Lancashire at one of Fleetwood's oldest surviving pubs on the harbour front. Worsthorne, Lancaster, Moorhouse's and Reedley Hallows are among the breweries that can be found behind the wood-panelled bar, with an excellent selection of seafood dishes to choose from if you get peckish.

Forest Green Rovers

Fact box
Nickname – The Green
Colours – Green and black
Ground – The New Lawn
Built in – 1889
Capacity – 5,141

Introduction

In 2017 Forest Green Rovers took the Football League by storm after banning beef burgers and meat pies from its cafeterias to establish itself as the world's first all-vegan football club. Its owner, Dale Vince, an eco-warrior millionaire who made his fortune by selling renewable electricity to the national grid, rolled out an environmentally friendly revolution in The Green's quiet corner of the Cotswolds. The club is now powered entirely by green energy, and the team plies its trade on an organic pitch maintained by a 'mowbot' that uses energy harnessed from the sun. But as honourable as their efforts may be, the 'vegan army' rarely escape the taunts of travelling fans who chant 'where's your sausage rolls?' and such in derision. A popular response is, 'I'd rather be vegan than in bread'. Or something to that effect.

What to eat and where to eat it

- ### Egypt Mill

  Kick back and enjoy the best of the Cotswolds on the Nailsworth Stream banks at the historic Egypt Mill, a riverside corn mill dating as far back as the 14th century. Inside, flagstone floors, exposed beams and quirky industrial objets d'art provide an idyllic setting for lunch, but for the best experience dine al fresco among the water and greenery, where a toasted ham and rarebit 'croque madame' is served with a free-range fried egg to make a perfect pre-match bite.

- ### William's Food Hall & Oyster Bar

  With a food market vibe, William's has long been regarded as the jewel in Nailsworth's gastronomic crown. Born out of a traditional food shop that used to sell fresh fish from a marble slab, as well as rabbits, fowls and pheasants which would hang from the roof, the deli still retains a fresh feel, with seafood out on display along with veg and artisanal produce. Share half a dozen Portland pearl rock oysters or Sicilian style mussels along with a lovely glass of house white.

- ### Wild Garlic

  Embrace your inner vegan at the two-AA rosette restaurant Wild Garlic in the heart of Nailsworth. The bistro serves a full vegan menu alongside some superb meat options. Kick off with cauliflower soup served with cauliflower bhaji before taking a pick between wild mushroom spaghetti or an aubergine, date and almond tagine for the main course. In the summer, Cossack Square's terrace is open for punters to eat outside amid the local flora and fauna.

What to drink and where to drink it

- **The Village Inn**

  You don't get beer served much fresher than the stuff brewed right under the bar at The Village Inn. Home to Keep Brewing, the pub is ideally located for a pre- or post-match sampling of the local ale, with four to try, ranging from a zesty pale ale through to the dark and stormy Odyssey brew. They even let you bring your own food or takeaway meals from the chip shop next door.

- **Waterloo House**

  Based in a beautiful old bank building, the Waterloo House is a recently reopened pub with a keen focus on serving local ales and food sourced from local vendors. Tuck into several hand-pulled beers from Stroud Brewery in the contemporary-chic bar, with a good food selection also available if you start to feel a little peckish.

- **Stroud Brewery Bar**

  One to plan ahead for, but Stroud Brewery Bar is well worth a visit if you can make time for it before the game. Since opening in 2006, the owners have championed organic and sustainable brewing and undoubtedly share the same eco stance as their local football club. Take a walk down the Thames and Severn Canal towpath from Stroud train station to enjoy their beer and other local drinks along with wood-fired pizzas.

Fulham

Fact box
Nickname – The Cottagers
Colours – White
Ground – Craven Cottage
Built in – 1896
Capacity – 19,359

Introduction

Steeped in history, Craven Cottage is a ground you just love to visit. With its wooden seats, riverside setting and elegant red-brick Edwardian turnstiles it is a glimpse into football as it used to be. On the grounds of a cottage built by the aristocrat William Craven, there remains to this day a cottage-like structure at the intersection between the Johnny Haynes Stand and the Putney End. Its namesake pie, which was popular among the people living in modest surroundings, could well have been a favourite of Craven's father, who was born to a poor family in Appletreewick in North Yorkshire before moving to London to make his fortune, becoming Lord Mayor of London in 1610. Today you can buy a Craven Cottage Pie at the ground, enjoying the familiar potato toppings within a shortcrust case or, as many like to call it, a pie within a pie.

What to eat and where to eat it

- **River Café**

  Not to be confused with the more upmarket River Café in Hammersmith, this is the greasy spoon close enough to Parsons Green to feel the rumbling of tube trains go by as you tuck into your full English. An endangered species among the increasingly gastro-chic breakfast scene, you know where you stand with this place.

- **Putney Pies**

  Purveyors of the 'finest pies in the land', Putney Pies and The Vault is an idyllic eating and drinking spot on the River Thames banks. Mini beef wellingtons are served up for starters with a selection of pies, pot pies, and bangers and mash for mains. Local beers from The Vault can be enjoyed al fresco next to the river.

- **MaGoa**

  Transport yourself to Goa's tropical climes in the hands of a third-generation restaurant still using grandma's old recipes. A mix of Portuguese and Indian flavours combine to make such dishes as hakka prawns, kale and cabbage pakora, and murgh mirchi walla. The house biryanis are also to die for.

What to drink and where to drink it

- **The Eight Bells**

  Find a proper pub next to a proper café next to a proper bookshop, all within a short stroll of a proper underground station at Putney Bridge, which is also, conveniently, the best stop for Craven Cottage. A good range of ales and pre-wrapped butties can be found at The Eight Bells, where crowds often spill out on to the street on matchdays.

- **Duke on the Green**

  Home to Fulham FC between 1889 and 1891, Parsons Green is an affluent area of London, home to many bistros, bridge clubs and beauty salons, but also good pubs. The pick of the bunch is Duke on the Green, which serves a good selection of ales in a typically refined setting.

- **The Crabtree**

  A popular spot during The Boat Race, this riverside pub with a quaint Victorian interior and one of the best beer gardens in west London is the perfect place to unwind after the game. Outside the winter months there are Orchard BarBQ grills at the weekend, offering a banging burger to go with your pint.

Gillingham

Fact box
Nickname – The Gills
Colours – Blue
Ground – Priestfield Stadium
Built in – 1893
Capacity – 11,582

Introduction

The history of Gillingham and the origins of its football club are best observed by getting off the train one stop before the central station at Chatham, where the historic dockyard gives a glimpse of a town once dominated by a thriving maritime industry. At one time, more than ten thousand people worked in the dockyard in a port that was at the forefront of shipbuilding, and industrial and architectural technology. The local football club was founded just down the road in 1893 when New Bromton FC received an unceremonious drubbing from local big boys, Woolwich Arsenal FC. Today you can enjoy a hearty lunch in The Wagon Shop Canteen, with a 'workshop' menu that includes 'doorstep' sandwiches, hot Kentish pies, cakes and delicious Kentish ice cream.

What to eat and where to eat it

- **Tracie's Café**

  Located next to an old Royal Navy dockyard, a military barracks and a Napoleonic fort, Tracie's Café might well be the most guarded café in Britain from a historical standpoint. And for a good reason. Its 'deluxe breakfast' would have put a smile on the face of Bonaparte himself if he were still around today, with the full mashings served alongside toast or fried slice with a mug of tea or coffee.

- **The Wagon Stop Canteen**

  Serving hearty 'doorstep' sandwiches and hot Kentish pies out of an old goods carriage in the middle of Chatham's historic dockyard is The Wagon Stop Canteen, where you'll find a range of local foods which can be either taken away or eaten alongside the locomotives. It also leaves you well placed to hit up the first pub if you feel so inclined.

- **The Pumproom**

  Packed to the rafters with locally sourced artisan foods, The Pumproom in the historic dockyards is a great spot to enjoy produce from the Garden of England, with a wide range of Mickey Mcguire's cheese, cured meats and drinks. Enjoy Kentish cider, English wine and craft gin from its very own Copper Rivet Distillery in the old industrial space.

What to drink and where to drink it

- **Nelson Brewery**

Set in the heart of the birthplace of HMS *Victory*, which is best known for her role as Lord Nelson's flagship at the Battle of Trafalgar, the admiral's namesake brewery has been pumping out premium Kentish ales since 1995. Formerly The Flagship Brewery, it now sells several enticing beers, such as Admiral IPA, Midshipman Dark Mild and Spanker.

- **The Cannon**

Well worth a visit on a sunny day, The Cannon is a decent, honest boozer in Brompton with a welcoming atmosphere and superb beer garden. Located on a Victorian terrace in the old Brompton Garrison, there are two bars, a pool table and usually a bit of sport on TV.

- **The Napier Arms**

Visually striking, The Napier Arms is an end-of-a-terrace pub dating back to the mid-19th century. Steeped in history, this is where the original Gillingham FC committee met and formed the club, originally known as New Brompton FC, in 1894.

Grimsby Town

Fact box
Nickname – The Mariners
Colours – Black and white
Ground – Blundell Park
Built in – 1899
Capacity – 9,052

Introduction

Once home to the world's largest fishing port, time was when a tenth of the fish consumed across the United Kingdom was landed at Grimsby. After The Haven was dredged in the late 18th century, the town proliferated as imports of iron, timber, wheat, hemp and flax moved through its docks, with wharves and warehouses erected for their storage. It wasn't until the arrival of the railway in 1848 that fish became its primary industry, with direct links to Billingsgate Market in London allowing fresh 'Grimsby fish' to gain renown nationwide. Such was the success that at its peak in the 1950s, trawlermen became known as 'three-day millionaires', owing to the short time they would have onshore to spend their hard-earned takings. Folk singer Mike Waterson wrote a song about them on his album *For Pence and Spicy Ale*. He noted their unique fishermen's suits with ruck-back jackets, padded shoulders, wide lapels and flared trousers, as well as their tendency to work like horses but spend like asses.

What to eat and where to eat it

- **The Pea Bung**

  Fresh fish doesn't get much fresher than Grimsby cod served just metres away from The Pea Bung docks. Serving the locals since 1883, it is known for its friendly faces, exceptional value and top-quality produce, and if you're popping through in December you'll even get to try their famous battered sprouts.

- **The Barge**

  A day out in a maritime town is a day wasted if you don't take the opportunity to have a bite to eat in a floating restaurant. Serving good-quality pub grub along with the local staple, fish and chips, there's no better place to find your sea legs.

- **The Smokehouse Kitchen**

  As well as being famous for its fish, Grimsby has one other gastronomic claim to fame: Adam Richman – aka Man Vs Food – as one of the football club's shareholders. After becoming familiar with the club on a flight home from the UK, he officially became involved in the partly fan-run club in 2020. You can pay homage to the eating-challenge king at The Smokehouse Kitchen near Grimsby Town station.

What to drink and where to drink it

- **Docks Beers**

  Take a pew among the mash tuns, barrels and other miscellaneous brewing equipment in the Docks Beers taproom, where you can work your way through a variety of cask, keg and canned beers brewed right where you sit. At four per cent ABV the Humber Bitter is a good session ale. Try Blood, Sweat and Tears if you're looking for something fruitier.

- **Message in a Bottle**

  Operating a small weekend bar on the side of a specialist bottle shop, Message in a Bottle is an independent shop that supports independent, award-winning microbreweries from across the county. Usually serving an Axholme pale ale or special reserve on tap, there is also the option of a Lincolnshire gin and tonic or even a local rum to try for anyone interested.

- **No. 1 Pub**

  A 'train pub not a chain pub', the No. 1 is a glorious find at the end of the line in Cleethorpes' historic station on the North Promenade. Serving ales from across Lincolnshire, you can tuck into a Batemans, Axholme or Horncastle as you wait for your train home; just be sure to keep an eye on the time.

Harrogate Town

Fact box
Nickname – Sulphurites
Colours – Yellow and black
Ground – Wetherby Road
Built in – 1920
Capacity – 5,000

Introduction

There are two things in Britain that, over the years, have become synonymous with three o'clock: football matches and afternoon teas, and although similarities between the two are hard to come by, they actually exist to serve similar purposes. The former, you see, was initially a church construct brought in to keep people out of the pubs when the Factory Act of 1850 dictated that workers were not to work any later than 2pm on a Saturday, while the latter was brought about in 1870 by Anna Maria Russell, 7th Duchess of Bedford, to fill the long gap between luncheon and dinner that left her feeling peckish mid-afternoon. So while one was brought in to stave off thirstiness, the other was created to stave off hunger – not that you will want to do either on a trip to Harrogate, widely considered to be the capital of high tea in one of Yorkshire's five spa towns.

What to eat and where to eat it

- **Bettys Café Tea Rooms**

  Not a regular haunt among football fans, granted, yet Bettys is an institution in Harrogate and warrants a quick pit stop on any visit, even if it's for a pastry and pikelet selection for breakfast. Served alongside a croissant and pain au chocolat, the savoury treat is essentially a flattened crumpet and goes well with a generous knob of butter.

- **Yorkshire Tapas**

  Visit the guys who eat Yorkshire, sleep Yorkshire, cut them open and they bleed gravy types at their famous Yorkshire Tapas restaurant on Montpellier Parade. Their modern twist on grazing-style dishes includes Yorkshire wraps, Bradford curry house masala and a to-die-for Yorkshire Blue cheese fondue served with a bucket of bakery bread.

- **Major Tom's Social**

  Ever fancied sitting down to dinner over a game of Jenga? Well, your prayers have been answered by Major Tom and his retro-fitted Social diner, which also specialises in stone-baked pizza, local beer flights and Pac-Man machines. The outlet's meatball and grana padano pizza is perfect after a long day out, and pairs well with a Northern Monk IPA.

What to drink and where to drink it

- **The Little Ale House**

  Set up by husband-and-wife team Rich and Danni to recreate a rustic country pub atmosphere in Harrogate town centre, The Little Ale House is a homespun haven of real ale, pork pies and cosiness. Kegs are stacked behind a glass screen, while there's a well-stocked little gin shelf with handmade and local spirits.

- **Harrogate Tap**

  A historic pub in the last remaining part of the original 1862 train station, the Harrogate Tap is housed in a charming building consisting of a long bar and a separate snug overlooking platform 1. Find beers from local Black Sheep, Kirkstall and Ilkley breweries.

- **The Fat Badger**

  Expect a cordial welcome at The Fat Badger, where you can knock back smooth, silky pints of Timothy Taylors and Copper Dragon in traditional beer mugs. You'll also find beers from Roosters of Harrogate, including Sawtooth and Tropical Assassin.

Huddersfield Town

> **Fact box**
> Nickname – The Terriers
> Colours – Blue and white
> Ground – The John Smith's Stadium
> Built in – 1994
> Capacity – 24,121

Introduction

In March 2017, two Yorkshire giants met to create a steak pie that would make all others quiver in their packaging at its mere mention. Combining the classic hot-water pastry of Huddersfield's Jones Pies with slow-cooked British beef and Henderson's Relish of Sheffield to give it a unique savoury tang, the White Rose institutions gave birth to an innovation not seen since roast dinners were wrapped in giant Yorkshire puddings to make the northern equivalent of Mexico's burrito (see *Leeds United*). Shortly after, Jones's, which was started in the back of a butcher's shop in 1988 and grew predominantly through word of mouth, became the pie suppliers to The John Smith's Stadium, with the club's official press release making a note of its commitment to working with local suppliers. Alongside Henderson's, Jones's also works with local millers Bradshaws, blends curry spices in Bradford (see *Bradford City*) and uses ales from Osset Brewery in its steak and ale pie. But it is their cold selection that has won them particular acclaim, having scooped awards for the best pork pie in the country on numerous occasions.

You might even find one made with a Yorkshire Blue from the highly regarded Shepherds Purse creamery in Thirsk if you are lucky.

What to eat and where to eat it

- **Northern Tea House**

  Occupying the intersection between fashion and food, the Northern Tea House is a gastro-chic café on Huddersfield's fashionable King Street. It serves an excellent 'northern breakfast' consisting of the usual fare piled into a hot skillet, or stay on-brand with zesty smashed avocado on sourdough toast topped with crumbled feta.

- **Steve's at the Mill**

  Textile mills are a common sight around Huddersfield, with their iconic chimneys dotting the skyline. You can try a Jones Pie at the foot of one, courtesy of Steve's at the Mill, which also does a cracking roast meat sandwich, toasties and wraps.

- **The Sportsman**

  A warm plate of pies, peas, mash and gravy awaits you at The Sportsman, where you can pick from a range of steak and port, 'moo and blue' and curry goat pies, among others. Wash it down with a real ale from a handful of local breweries.

What to drink and where to drink it

- **Head of Steam**

  With station frontage described by John Betjeman as 'the most splendid in England', you should be in no rush to leave the Grade I building once described as 'the only important Victorian railway station in the West Riding'. Decked out in old waiting room furnishings, the Head of Steam provides the perfect excuse to stay put and get acquainted with some local ales.

- **Magic Rock Brewing**

  Inspired by Yorkshire's local beer heritage and the vibrant craft beer scene in the US, Magic Rock Brewing is widely revered as one of the most exciting new brewers on the block. Its spacious brewery taproom supplies the freshest beers across ten taps and five cask lines.

- **The Grove**

  Nine cask ale pumps and a resplendent row of keg taps sit proudly on The Grove's central bar, with beers from Thornbridge, Kirkstall and Northern Monk breweries a regular feature. There is also a spacious beer garden out back if, perchance, the sun shows itself.

Hull City

Fact box
Nickname – The Tigers
Colours – Amber and black
Ground – KCOM Stadium
Built in – 2001
Capacity – 25,400

Introduction

Competition over the best deep-fried foods is hot in the north of England and even hotter north of that, but Hull has a pretty strong claim in the shape of its native 'pattie'. Dating back to the 1800s when they were sold as a cheap alternative to fish patties, the deep-fried snack encompasses mashed potato with sage, creating a jagged, golden exterior that gives way to a steaming, soft, herb-speckled heart. Still popular in most fish and chip shops, there was a time when the women who crafted the snacks were affectionately known as 'pattie slappers' due to the arduous process of slapping countless discs of potato with seasoning. Today it makes for the perfect pre- or post-match snack served alongside a mound of chip-shop chips doused in salt, vinegar and another local favourite, American chip spice.

What to eat and where to eat it

- **Smithy's**
Home to the best pattie in Hull, Smithy's of Beverley Road is a whitewashed annexed chippy on the side of a pub. And if that sounds like perfection, wait until you taste its deep-fried herby potato treats. Wrap it in a breadcake, smother it in peas or take it with a mound of chips, not forgetting to generously sauce.

- **Humber Fish Co.**
Visit the 2017 City of Culture's unique cultural quarter at Humber Fish Co. in the heart of the Fruit Market. Seafaring objects decoratively adorn the ceilings and counter spaces, with an extensive menu offering seabass, halibut and an enticing seafood diablo.

- **The Old House**
Take a trip down Hull's old cobblestone roads to find The Old House, which serves up a delightful array of Yorkshire dishes in one of the city's oldest domestic buildings. Try the smoked haddock Scotch egg, locally sourced wagyu beef or any dish that comes with chunky chips cooked in beef dripping.

What to drink and where to drink it

- **Taphouse Brewpub**

  Offering close to 40 draught craft beers, lagers and ciders displayed on a theatre board-style creation, Taphouse Brewpub is undoubtedly a fine place to start on any given matchday. Located in the heart of the marina, the old industrial space is also home to Yorkshire Brewing Company and Bone Machine Brew Co., which have created such delights as Brewculture, Garden of Death and the Nordic Barbarian.

- **Fretwells**

  Styled as a cosy real ale pub, Fretwells is another Old Town staple that has been built to fit within its surroundings rather than around them. Six handpumps serve a range of beers from across the country, but Cathead Brewery ales are the ones you really ought to try, brewed right here on the High Street.

- **Wm Hawkes**

  Despite only being open since 2012, Wm Hawkes – housed in a former gunmaker's shop – has all the hallmarks of a pub from the 18th century. Chairs with decorative metal backs, wood panels and old tankards fill the room, which makes for an excellent place to hide in the event of a thrashing.

Ipswich Town

Fact box
Nickname – The Tractor Boys
Colours – Blue and White
Ground – Portman Road
Built in – 1884
Capacity – 30,311

Introduction

If there's one thing that you can rely on when driving down East Anglian A-roads, it's that traffic will invariably be held up by a slow-moving tractor at some point. Blessed with a bounty of agricultural land, the 'backside of Britain' is a vast tapestry of vegetable, fruit and floral fields, with dairy farms, hayfields and tree farms adding to its vibrant output. This agricultural link is preserved in the local football club's nickname 'The Tractor Boys', which was reportedly bestowed upon them by Birmingham City, who taunted fans with 'no noise from The Tractor Boys' when they were losing away in the 1998/99 season. It has stuck ever since and as well as denoting the town's notorious congestion problems, it also points to the bounty of produce that can be found in its cafés and restaurants, which are lucky enough to have proximity to the best of both land and sea.

What to eat and where to eat it

- **Cult Café**

  Old furnishings and bags of character will greet you at this bohemian indoor/outdoor café on the harbour front, which is ideally placed to kick off proceedings. 'Fat boy pancakes' and a range of baps will help line the stomach for early birds, but aim for the deli counter for a sample of locally sourced, homemade treats. The 'jacked-up Reuben' bagel or the 'tend to blue' flatbread pair particularly well with a nice cold beer.

- **Biryani Hut**

  An Ipswich food market stalwart and local favourite, the Biryani Hut can be found plying its trade every Tuesday, Thursday, Friday and Saturday in the heart of town. The Bangladeshi caterers will whip up a choice of biryanis or wraps with a samosa and drink for less than a tenner, with a pot of curry sauce to boot. For those with deeper pockets, the lamb sheesh starter accompanied with an excellent hot chicken biryani is a real touch that will leave you comfortably warm for the game.

- **The Forge Kitchen**

  In a land where locally sourced ingredients are not hard to come by, The Forge Kitchen's 'as nature intended' philosophy is undoubtedly a commendable one. Copper abounds, and heavy metal furnishings give the appearance of a blacksmith's workshop with smoke scents emanating from the smoker, furnace and hanger. The meaty menu includes small plates of smoked beef bonbons and pork belly bites with apple chutney, followed by a range of steaks, burgers or 'feastings' for those with an appetite.

What to drink and where to drink it

- **Briarbank Brewing Company**

  With ales brewed on-site and pumped mere metres up to the bar above, you can rest assured of a fresh pint in the Briarbank Brewing Company, where pictures of old Ipswich adorn the walls of the modern taproom. Repurposed wooden barrels support rows of tables, with beer menus on hand to help punters navigate their ample range.

- **Dove Street Inn**

  A real ale drinker's haven, the Dove Street Inn packs in everything one could wish for from a 'proper' boozer, with warm, rustic vibes that lend themselves to an afternoon holed up with a broadsheet newspaper in your hands and your dog at your feet. Beer festivals pop up periodically but fear not if your timings don't coincide, this place has a superb selection year round.

- **Arcade Street Tavern**

  With a striking façade and trendy interior, the Arcade Street Tavern makes for a perfect spot to unwind and reflect post-match. The beer selection is met in kind by an equally impressive array of gins and wines. Widescreen TVs in cosy upstairs rooms show live sport on TV, with resident DJs seeing in the night later on.

Leeds United

Fact box
Nickname – The Whites
Colours – White
Ground – Elland Road
Built in – 1897
Capacity – 37,890

Introduction

Few clubs have a history so intertwined with their local pub than Leeds United. Born out of Hunslet and then Leeds City FC, the club inherited a ground located in a part of town once owned by Bentley's Brewery, where they plied their trade at the Old Peacock Ground, named after a local pub standing opposite the playing field. The club was nicknamed The Peacocks and it is said that their first colours of royal blue with yellow edgings were derived from the eponymous bird. Today the pub still stands, serving beers from the local Ossett Brewery just a few miles down the road. You may even find the odd local willing to regale you with stories of how Jack Charlton used to slip into the boozer for a pint before a game with his full kit on, although such claims are hard to substantiate.

What to eat and where to eat it

- **Yorkshire Wrap Company**

  Trademarked purveyors of the Yorkshire equivalent to the Mexican burrito, this café is not one you will want to miss on any journey to the county's principal city. Tucked away among the food stalls of Kirkgate Market, the Yorkshire Wrap Company serves slow-cooked meats in a Yorkshire pudding wrap with gravy and all the trimmings. Early birds will also be able to sample the breakfast wrap, with the contents of a full English delivered in the same style.

- **Bundobust**

  Tuck into vegetarian Indian street food and craft beer amid bare brick and wooden benches and tables at the funky Bundobust on Mill Hill. Okra fries, 'Bundo chaat' and Mumbai's favourite burger, the 'vada pav', are all worth sampling, but for an authentic taste of the north order the 'raghda pethis', a spicy mushy pea and potato cake topped with onion and tamarind chutney.

- **Friends of Ham**

  Make new acquaintances with some of the finest European and local charcuterie at Friends of Ham, an idyllic pit stop before the long journey home on New Station Road. Set boards include the British meat plate, a smoked mariscos selection and Ham's favourite cheese board, but the real treats can be found among the small dishes, where the king of Spanish ham is sourced from pigs fed on a diet of acorns before being cured for four years.

What to drink and where to drink it

- **The Brewery Tap**

  Despite having a proud brewing history, the city was left bereft of beer makers when Tetley's called time on their city-centre brewery in 2008 after 186 years. Thankfully, it wasn't long before Leeds Brewery brought the tradition back, selling their wares out of a brewery tap just a short walk from the station. Leeds pale is a well-rounded IPA, but Midnight Bell is among the most distinctive of their brews.

- **The Hop**

  Take a walk through one of Leeds' best-kept secrets to find one of its best pubs in The Hop, a watering hole hidden beneath the train station and serving a range of Yorkshire beers along with pies and pizza. To get there you will need to walk through Granary Wharf, where the River Aire flows beneath the railway arches creating an eerie experience.

- **Northern Monk Refectory**

  Another upstart putting Leeds back on the map as a brewery centre, Northern Monk is nationally regarded for its beers that combine traditional monastic brewing values with a progressive approach to ingredients and techniques. Their Refectory is located in the outskirts of town in Elland Road's direction and is well worth a post- or pre-match visit.

Leicester City

Fact box
Nickname – The Foxes
Colours – Blue
Ground – King Power Stadium
Built in – 2002
Capacity – 32,261

Introduction

Twenty miles north-east of Leicester, with a population that would comfortably fit into the King Power Stadium, lies Britain's Rural Capital of Food. Home to Stilton-producing farms (see *Peterborough United*), the third-oldest recorded market in the country and one of the most interesting food festivals in the world, Melton Mowbray is an artisanal hero on the gastronomic map of Britain and a firm favourite of one half of the Two Fat Ladies, Clarissa Dickson Wright, who campaigned for its certified status. But the chief feather in its cap is, of course, the famed pork pie (see *Crewe Alexandra*), which came about due to a need to preserve pork and provide a portable snack for local farmhands and huntsmen, hence the thick, tightly-sealed crust. These days it is practically unheard of to take a picnic out that doesn't contain a pork pie, but for it to be the genuine article with Protected Geographical Indication (PGI) status it must be made in Melton Mowbray. Unfortunately, they are in woefully short supply in Leicester, but you will find pies from Brockleby's on sale near the King Power. As one eager review notes, 'I have travelled to over 60 rugby and football

grounds and no pie is even close to their taste and quality';
they are 'far superior to the providers currently at Leicester
City Football Club'.

What to eat and where to eat it

- **Mrs Bridges Tea Rooms**
  Dubbed 'the time warp street which remains largely
  unchanged' by the *Leicester Mercury*, Loseby Lane in the
  historic market quarter looks the same today as it did 50
  years ago. Named after a Leicester burgess who owned
  land in the city in the 14th century, it is home to a lovely
  tea room serving homemade cooked breakfasts that can
  be enjoyed indoors or in the courtyard.

- **W. Archer & Son**
  Finding Melton Mowbray pork pies in Leicester is
  disappointingly difficult, but you have a good chance
  of getting your hands on one at butchers W. Archer &
  Son near the King Power. They stock Brockleby's which,
  according to one punter, are 'far superior' to anything you
  will get in the ground.

- **The Good Earth**
  Tucked away in Free Lane, off Halford Street, lies one of
  Leicester's hidden gems in the shape of The Good Earth
  restaurant. This family-run vegetarian place displays old
  farmhouse odds and ends on the walls and exposed ceiling
  beams, giving it a country feel in the heart of the city centre.

What to drink and where to drink it

- **The Ale Wagon**

  A pub that keeps beer as well as it makes it is well worth a visit in my book, and that is precisely what you will find at The Ale Wagon, where several generations of the famous Hoskins family have mastered the craft of cellarmanship. Antique bottles from the aforementioned brewery are also generally in good stock and well worth a try.

- **The West End Brewery**

  Decorated from wall to ceiling in beer pump clips, the cosy West End Brewery is Leicester's first city-centre brewpub stocking its own beers, along with a countless number of others. The door to the brewery is directly behind the bar, giving anything on tap a freshness-guaranteed stamp.

- **The Black Horse**

  Based just moments away from where William Everard brewed his first-ever pint in 1849, The Black Horse of the same brewery is an idyllic place to end the day in the company of a Tiger beer and either a coal fire or a suntrap beer garden, depending on the season. Grab a dimpled beer mug of fries or onion rings if you feel peckish.

Leyton Orient

Introduction

In the early hours of every morning, as the rest of the capital sleeps, London's wholesale markets are operating in full swing as produce from across the country is traded by merchants on an enormous scale. Long regarded as the linchpin of Britain's diverse agricultural output, they provide fishers, farmers and floriculturists with vital market access and have supported industries from across the country which otherwise may never have taken off (see *Grimsby, Morecambe*). In recent years decentralisation has created many new (old) markets operating on London's fringes, namely the New Covent Garden Market, new Billingsgate Market and the behemoth New Spitalfields Market based in Leyton, and further changes could be afoot. The City of London Corporation wants to move all markets under one roof in the former Barking Reach power station, freeing up old sites for housing and office development. But one site could be preserved for something rather special, making way for the new Museum of London, where the history of the capital's trading relationships will be preserved.

THE GREAT PIE REVOLT

What to eat and where to eat it

- **The Wild Goose Bakery**

  Celebrate the exotic fruit and vegetables that make its nearby wholesale market renowned at The Wild Goose Bakery, where an ever-changing menu reflects the seasonality at the heart of all the Bakery does. Enjoy a locally roasted coffee as you peruse its blackboard; you are guaranteed to find something you will like.

- **The Sunflower Café & Crêperie**

  Styled like an American diner in hornet's clothing, The Sunflower Café & Crêperie is a lively neighbourhood haunt offering up soulful foods and drinks guaranteed to put a smile on your face. Try one of its savoury crêpes washed down with an exotic fruit smoothie.

- **Deeney's**

  The saying in Leyton goes, 'you haven't lived until you've tried a haggis toastie from Deeney's', and I'd be inclined to agree. The famous 'Hamish Macbeth' includes the signature Scottish pudding topped with bacon, cheddar cheese, rocket, caramelised onions, mustard and – if you wish – a fried egg, and is simply delightful.

What to drink and where to drink it

- **Gravity Well**

  Microbreweries are not in short supply in this part of London, but there's no better place to kick off your day than at a brewery that specialises in hazy, hoppy New England-style pales and IPAs. The Gravity Well's taproom is located in the railway arch next door to Leyton Midland Road overground station. Planetary Alignment and Termination Shock are pretty special.

- **Solvay Society**

  Belgian-born, London-brewed, the Solvay Society brings the best of Europe to Leyton with barrel-aged beer, Witbier and Tripel among the wide range of continental ales on offer. The outlet is paired with the local Yard Sale Pizza. Create a pre-match meal of champions with The Maestro accompanied by a Bière Du Hainault.

- **The Leyton Star**

  A rustic interior at The Leyton Star may seem inviting, but take a few steps further and you will find its lively outdoor terraced area complete with darts, table football and the arcade classic Street Fighter. Battle it out to see if you can make the wall of fame with a high score.

Lincoln City

Fact box
Nickname – The Imps
Colours – Red and white
Ground – LNER Stadium
Built in – 1894
Capacity – 10,120

Introduction

It's our national breakfast, but if the results of a recent poll are to be believed, it could die out within a generation as health-conscious millennials ditch sausage, bacon and eggs for smashed avocado on sourdough toast. According to the survey, almost one in five Brits under 30 have never had a full English breakfast, with a quarter of respondents claiming they are 'too greasy' and 42 per cent saying they 'remind them of men in vests hanging around in transport cafés'. But the fry-up is an institution in Britain, protected by a learned society of Fellows and, indeed, a 'Fry-Up Police' on Twitter. As the king of the vest, Rab C. Nesbitt might say: 'It will take more than a group of wee flannel-arsed naebodies to change that.' Without the full English breakfast we might not have the same proliferation of glorious sausages that span the country in regional varieties. Along with the Cumberland (see *Carlisle United*), one of the most popular types is the Lincolnshire sausage, which uses the herb sage rather than the more peppery flavour balance found elsewhere, and contains meat which is chopped coarsely rather than mashed. Every year butchers from across the region head to the Lincolnshire Sausage Festival held in Lincoln Castle's grounds, where you will find a vast array of different artisan products and dishes to try to the foot-tapping tunes of the ultimate party band, the Cosmic Sausages. The dress code is casual and string vests are optional, but for heaven's sake, don't mention the avocado!

What to eat and where to eat it

- **Stokes High Bridge Café**

  Step back in time in a building that dates back to 1540, where Stokes High Bridge Café staff in period dress serve up an excellent full English consisting of Lincolnshire sausage and Lincolnshire home-cured bacon. They even cater for those pesky millennials with an avocado on sourdough breakfast.

- **Bunty's Tea Room**

  A triple-layered Lincolnshire sausage and smoked bacon sandwich awaits you at Bunty's Tea Room halfway up the dastardly Steep Hill. You can also try traditional Lincolnshire Plum Bread served with mature cheddar cheese and a caramelised red onion chutney.

- **Browns Pie Shop**

  You won't find a better place in the whole of Lincolnshire to finish off a long day out than in the snug cellar restaurant of Browns Pie Shop. Using locally sourced produce and locally caught game, you will find a host of exemplary pies and pickles made in-house by the Browns chefs, including a 'beef and Lincolnshire ale' pie, a 'mixed Lincolnshire game' pie and a 'pork, black pudding and apple' pie.

What to drink and where to drink it

- **The Treaty of Commerce**

  Step off the train and into The Treaty of Commerce, a pub named after an Anglo-French free trade agreement that ended tariffs on items such as wine and brandy. Supplying beers from Batemans Brewery of Skegness, this is among the oldest and certainly cosiest pubs in the town, which is no mean feat for Lincoln.

- **The Jolly Brewer**

  You will find plenty of cheer at The Jolly Brewer and a good selection of little-known beers from around Yorkshire, Lincolnshire and the Midlands. Welbeck Abbey, Horncastle and Pheasantry Brewery can often be found on tap, with live music on in the evenings and a generous-sized beer garden.

- **The Dog and Bone**

  Old timber beams support The Dog and Bone's exposed brick bar, with books and beer tankards taking pride of place around its varnished frame. Batemans regularly feature on tap as well as beers from Blue Monkey Brewery and B&T. Kick back with a board game in front of a roaring coal fire.

Liverpool

Fact box
Nickname – The Reds
Colours – Red
Ground – Anfield
Built in – 1884
Capacity – 53,394

Introduction

Being a historic port town, Liverpool has long been influenced by faraway lands. Home to the oldest Chinatown in Europe, the city was among the first to experience exotic Asian cuisines brought over on the Alfred Holt & Co. shipping line from Shanghai in the 1850s. Its native dish, Scouse, is derived from lobscouse, a stew commonly eaten by sailors throughout northern Europe, and you'll find some of the best Nordic cuisines Britain has to offer in the city thanks to long-standing nautical ties. The cuisines of the Caribbean and Africa have outlived the port, the remains of which are now part of the UNESCO as a maritime mercantile city. The port's legacy has been to leave a culinary melting pot of cuisines from across the world, often best enjoyed when they get fused – usually down at the chippy!

What to eat and where to eat it

- **Chris's Chippy**

  A trip to Liverpool is not complete without tasting the city's most proud fusion, salt and pepper chips. Owing to its high density of Chinese chippies, it is not uncommon to walk away from any fish bar with a portion of 'siumai' with your fish supper. But if you're just passing through, the unique concoction of onion, green pepper, chilli and salt with chips is a must.

- **SKAUS**

  Celebrate Liverpool's historical Nordic connection in the Baltic Triangle at a restaurant that combines Scandinavian culture with seasonal cooking and Scouse hospitality. Featuring Swedish meatballs that will put any IKEA café to shame and 'smørrebrød' that will make the reddest-cheeked Dane blush, this is an ideal place to shelter during the winter months.

- **Yuet Ben**

  They say that even though Liverpool has the biggest Chinese Arch outside China and the oldest Chinese expatriate community in the world, Yuet Ben has become *the* cornerstone of Sino-Scouse relations over the past 50 years. Founded in 1968 by Yuh Ho Yau of Yantai in Shandong, the restaurant remains in family hands to this day, with daughter Theresa and her husband Terry Lim carrying on the unique style of northern Chinese cuisine.

What to drink and where to drink it

- ### The Philharmonic Dining Rooms

  Dazzling and flamboyant, 'the most ornate pub in England', known as 'The Phil' to the locals, is an art nouveau watering hole based in the heart of the 'Knowledge Quarter' and just a stone's throw from Liverpool's Philharmonic Hall, from which it takes its name. Built in the style of a gentleman's club, it has an immediate 'wow' factor which is further enhanced by a good selection of food and drink.

- ### Peter Kavanagh's

  Listed by CAMRA as a historic pub with an interior of national importance, Peter Kavanagh's takes its name from its licensee for over 50 years (between 1897 and 1950), who fitted it out in a charming and idiosyncratic manner. You'll find everything from toy trains to penny-farthings dotted around the room, and an excellent real ale selection to boot.

- ### Ye Cracke

  If there's one thing you travel to Liverpool for – aside from the food and the football – it's the crack, and you'll find plenty of that in a bar that cares so dearly about it they decided to include it in their name. Frequented by John Lennon and his girlfriend Cynthia when they were at art school, as well as the Dissenters, it is renowned among Scousers and well worth checking out before catching the train home.

Luton Town

Fact box
Nickname – The Hatters
Colours – Orange
Ground – Kenilworth Road
Built in – 1905
Capacity – 10,356

Introduction

Home to one of the most multicultural populations in the UK, Luton is an unsung hero of Britain's fixation with worldly cuisines. In its historic indoor market, you will find modest stalls serving food from Korea, Africa, the Mediterranean, Thailand and even Trinidad and Tobago, along with a vast array of produce to cater for the town's diverse gastronomic taste buds. Halal butchers sit next to friendly fishmongers, a Thai grocery stall neighbours the Jamaican Cuisine Centre, and the nearby Caribbean food market sells some of the most delicious hot patties for lunch. Outside the market Bury Park suburb, the home of Kenilworth Road and Luton Town, is the heartland of the town's Asian population, and there are plenty of tasty treats from the subcontinent to be found for those who care to seek them out.

What to eat and where to eat it

- **Thai Bites**

  Tucked away in Luton's Market Hall, Thai Bites is a much-loved hidden gem among a plethora of tasty pre-match meal offerings. Boasting friendliness and authenticity in equal measure, the food stall will set you up for the day, with crispy chicken wings, beef panang and prawn tom yum soup the pick of the bunch.

- **Ambala**

  Stock up on pre-match treats at Asian confectionery shop Ambala, which is conveniently located on the approach to Kenilworth Road. Swap jelly babies for jalebis and bounties for barfis as you discover the often underexplored and underappreciated sweet dishes of the subcontinent. Their 'pista barfi', 'special ladoo' and, of course, 'baklava' are to die for.

- **Jay Raj**

  Post-match curry houses are in good supply in Luton, with several dotted on Dunstable Road connecting Kenilworth Road to the town centre. But if you want something really special, it is worth making the trip to Jay Raj in Stopsley, where you can indulge in a beautiful off-the-bone tandoori dish called 'jayraj lajawab' with Bombay aloo and kulcha naan.

What to drink and where to drink it

- **The Great Northern**

  Wedged between an easyHotel and an old hat factory, The Great Northern couldn't be more Luton Town if it tried. The tiny pub has the feel of an old parochial Irish pub, having remained untouched since the 1930s. Prepare to get that 'they don't make 'em like this anymore' feeling.

- **Bricklayers Arms**

  Dating back to 1824, the Bricklayers Arms is a historic pub with a wide selection of guest beers and a good range of Belgian bottled beers and ciders. Wooden barrels are propped on the top of the bar, with larger wine barrels dotted around the room. Two TVs show football if you fancy watching the early or late kick-offs.

- **The Bear Club**

  Unbeknown to many, Luton is home to one of the few surviving independent jazz record labels in England, and what better way to celebrate the sounds of old industrial centres than in its own jazz and blues bar, The Bear Club. Kick back with a beer as you join a small throng of people crowded cosily around the venue's intimate stage.

Manchester City

Introduction

Manchester City fans tend to have a lot to smile about these days. Bankrolled by Abu Dhabi wealth, they have become a mainstay at the top of the Premier League table, outgrowing their 'noisy neighbour' tag with the best talent money can buy. But it wasn't always that way. Back in the late 1980s, when City were wallowing in the Second Division, there wasn't much cheer to be found on the terraces of the old Maine Road stadium. Seven managers in ten years and a string of abject performances rather sucked the life out of their usually enigmatic fans, many of whom lamented a wasted decade for the club as United and Liverpool continued to dominate. But when computer analyst Frank Newton visited his mate in Leeds he discovered what would become the club's saviour in the unlikeliest of objects: an inflatable banana. He started a craze that took the home terraces by storm, with literally thousands visible on any given matchday. In his book *The Secret History of a Club that has no History*, Mike Devlin notes how the inflatable banana saved football for many City fans, who, of course, embellished the idea. It is said that for the opening fixture of the 1988/89 season the M62 was packed with inflatable-wielding motorists heading to Hull, with a toucan, a seven-foot golf club, a spitfire and a Red Baron all spotted en route.

What to eat and where to eat it

- **Maine Road Chippy**

  Take fish, chips and 'Manchester caviar', aka mushy peas, at the famous and long-standing Maine Road Chippy, a traditional, small, red-bricked building standing directly opposite the modern City of Manchester Stadium.

- **Solita**

  You've heard of the Big Mac, but did you know of its northern sister, the Big Manc? Available to try at Solita in the Northern Quarter, it consists of two juicy steak patties, lettuce, cheese and the restaurant's own secret sauce. Expect a stack twice the size of the original.

- **Elnecot**

  Try another civic speciality in the shape of the 'Manchester egg', a spin on the Scotch egg, at popular British small-plate bistro Elnecot. A pickled egg is coated in black pudding and sausage meat, topped with panko breadcrumbs and deep-fried until golden brown.

What to drink and where to drink it

- **The Runaway Brewery**

  Step off the train and duck under the railway tracks for a pint at The Runaway Brewery, a small-batch producer with a cosy mezzanine area for drinkers. A core range of pale ale, IPA, American brown and a smoked porter join seasonal specials and the odd collaboration.

- **Blackjack Brewery**

  The best suntrap beer garden in Manchester can be found at the Blackjack Brewery, where random pieces of pub furniture are assembled outside its railway arch brewery, and many an hour can be passed working through its long list of craft beers.

- **Alphabet**

  Do you love the smell of simcoe in the morning? Well, you'll love Alphabet's signature Charlie Don't Surf IPA, which will propel you atop a wave of citrus and peach with a 'more-than-moreish' flavour. Be sure to sample some of their pun-tastic special ales, including the Juice Springsteen, Moose Springsteen and Juice Willis.

Manchester United

Fact box
Nickname – The Red Devils
Colours – Red
Ground – Old Trafford
Built in – 1910
Capacity – 74,879

Introduction

As a club worth over £3 billion, many people may not realise that the area in which Manchester United ply their trade is among the ten per cent most deprived places in England, suffering unemployment problems, poor housing and low educational achievement. During the Covid-19 pandemic of 2020 and 2021, these inequalities were exacerbated and, with children forced to stay at home, there were grave concerns that many wouldn't get the same provisions as in school. Thankfully they received a lifeline in the shape of Manchester United forward Marcus Rashford, who successfully lobbied the government not once but twice to distribute vouchers to those in need. He also received the backing of hundreds of grassroots restaurants and cafés across the country who pledged to step in to help out. As meals were batch-cooked and lunch boxes were handed out, he took a moment to step back and tweet, 'Selflessness, kindness, togetherness, this is the England I know.'

What to eat and where to eat it

- **The Coffee House Café**

  Find a mural of the free school meal champion Marcus Rashford on the side of The Coffee House Café accompanied by the quote, 'take pride in knowing that your struggle will play the biggest role in your purpose'. A 'cheeky monster breakfast' from the café is well worth trying while you are there.

- **Lou Macari**

  Named after former Manchester United midfielder and proud Scot Lou Macari, this humble fish and chip joint is a regular haunt among home fans who turn up to pay homage to the football star and tuck into some top-quality nosh. Before joining The Red Devils, Macari was one of Celtic's so-called Quality Street Gang, the outstanding reserve team that included Kenny Dalglish and Danny McGrain.

- **The Drop Bar Café**

  Good food, good drinks and good vibes await at The Drop Bar Café, a Caribbean restaurant in the suburban district of Chorlton-cum-Hardy. Small plates of jerk chicken and jerk halloumi work well as aperitifs before getting stuck into main dishes such as curry goat, silver hake and prawn stew or grilled lamb chops washed down with a selection of delicious rum-based cocktails.

What to drink and where to drink it

- **The Lass O'Gowrie**

  Based in what was once one of the most impoverished areas of the city mainly populated by Irish immigrants, The Lass O'Gowrie is a smartly refurbished pub with a keen focus on local beers and good bar snacks. Despite its Irish origin, a Scottish landlord named the pub in honour of his favourite poem about a girl from Gowrie, now known as Perthshire.

- **The Knott**

  An impressive wall of nearly 20 beer taps can be found behind the bar at The Knott, where local brewery Wander Beyond gets a good show with a range of beers that pair perfectly with the pub's Neapolitan sourdough pizzas.

- **The Beer House**

  Not to be confused with its namesake equivalent in Manchester Victoria, The Beer House in Chorlton-cum-Hardy is a rustic micropub serving some glorious local and national ales in a cosy, intimate setting. Sit outside in the summer or dive into the snug in the winter months.

Mansfield Town

Fact box
Nickname – The Stags
Colours – Yellow and blue
Ground – Field Mill
Built in – 1861
Capacity – 9,186

Introduction

British beer adverts in the 1980s were as bonkers as they were brilliant. Burton-brewed Carling (see *Burton Albion*) used the line 'I bet he drinks Carling Black Label!' as they featured gravity-defying window cleaners and giant-squid-fighting fishermen, while Foster's humorously poked fun at a pub morris dance with a confused Aussie who quipped, 'Which one's Maurice?' But if the ads were barmy, the slogans were even barmier. Heineken sought to defy biology with the tag line 'Refreshes the parts other beers cannot reach', Carlsberg claimed it was 'Probably the best beer in the world' (see *Northampton Town*) and Courage courageously went with 'It's what your right arm's for!' But one that remains a beacon of a bygone golden era for British bitter hails from north Nottinghamshire, where a plucky brewery situated less than half a kilometre from Field Mill adopted the slogan 'Not much matches Mansfield.' As it happens, 'not much other than Wolverhampton matches Mansfield' would have been more apt after the brewery was taken over in 1999 and moved to the Midlands (see *Wolverhampton Wanderers*), before being demolished altogether in 2008 to make way for housing. It is said that when the brewery's brick chimney came down, it brought to an end part of the town's cultural heritage and officially marked the end of brewing in Mansfield. Or did it?

What to eat and where to eat it

- **Capo Lounge**

  A vibrant café with bizarre furnishings, the Capo Lounge is about as eccentric a place as you will find in Mansfield and makes for the perfect place to start a day in the town. The Anglo-American-inspired breakfast menu is extensive, offering a 'Brooklyn brunch', triple-stacked buttermilk pancakes with bacon and all the classic English staples.

- **Babuji's**

  Contenders for Britain's next fast-food sensation, Babuji's of Mansfield offers a range of fried chicken and burgers cooked in its house style as well as Indian curry cooked two ways. Choose from the Anglo-Indian versions most people are accustomed to, or from the home-style menu, billed as 'curry like they eat in India'.

- **Andwhynot Bar and Restaurant**

  And why not indeed. Finish the day in a contemporary restaurant sipping classic bitter and eating classically cooked, hearty British food. The homemade Scotch eggs with black pudding and a soft-boiled hen's egg are a touch if they have it on the menu, as is the locally sourced 'Mr Boot's hand-pressed steak and ale pie'.

What to drink and where to drink it

- **The Railway Inn**

  An incredible selection of beers awaits at the warm and welcoming Railway Inn pub at the back of Mansfield train station. Local ales from Dukeries, Full Mash and Pheasantry can often be found on tap to be enjoyed in the snug bar or out in the beer garden.

- **The Swan**

  Discover why 'not much matches Mansfield' at The Swan, where a pint of the smooth, creamy ale is available by the pint or the pitcher. The historic coaching inn dates back to the 1500s, making it one of the oldest pubs in town.

- **Prior's Well Brewery**

  Reviving Mansfield's proud brewing history, Prior's Well is a recently established microbrewery in the heart of the town with a splendid Victorian bar on site. Toast the renaissance with a pint of Citra, Incensed or Baby Wolf.

Middlesbrough

Fact box
Nickname – The Boro
Colours – Red
Ground – Riverside Stadium
Built in – 1995
Capacity – 34,742

Introduction

Although few towns would claim to have had their local gastronomy enhanced by fast-food outlets, Middlesbrough gave rise to its local delicacy, parmo, thanks to its takeaway shops that still cook up their own versions of the meaty treat in time-honoured fashion to this day. Consisting of a breaded cutlet of chicken or pork topped with a white béchamel sauce and cheese, the dish was first brought to the town by Nicos Harris, a chef with the American army who moved to Teesside after he was injured in France in the 1950s. His son-in-law, Caramello, still lives locally and, as of 2014, was continuing the family's proud parmo tradition. But the city is now its true guardian. As an enthusiast once said, 'If the parmo was a place, I'd like to think it'd be Middlesbrough. No nonsense, hard as nails, no airs and graces.'

What to eat and where to eat it

- **The Stottie Company**

  There are few meals this side of the North Sea that will set you up for the day like the full English stottie washed down with a barista hand-crafted coffee or mug of tea. Bacon, sausage, egg, hash brown, black pudding and a runny egg are crammed inside a stottie cake and will banish any pangs of hunger until well after the game.

- **Borge Restaurant**

  You'll have to travel north of the River Tees to get your hands on the parmo that was officially judged the best at the last World Parmo Championships. Borge Restaurant of Stockton has won the gong four times now for its chicken parmesan, which is well worth making a detour for.

- **Café Central Park**

  Celebrate or commiserate in Central Park's lively café, where, win or lose, you will find an electric atmosphere to boost your spirits. The menu includes a wide range of restaurant-quality parmos, including the 'hotshot parmesan' with a spicy topping finish, 'pulled pork parmo', and an old favourite 'spag bol parmo'.

What to drink and where to drink it

- **The Infant Hercules**

  If micropubs in repurposed retail spaces are your thing, then Middlesbrough's so-called solicitors' quarter is where you want to head before the game. The pick of the bunch is The Infant Hercules on Grange Road, which is named after William Gladstone's description of the town in 1862 after he witnessed the expansion of local industries. A good selection of ales is always on tap, with third ping tasting trays available.

- **Twisted Lip**

  Named as a 'rising star' in a recent Great British High Street competition, Baker Street in Middlesbrough's independent quarter is home to a variety of small businesses that will provide you with a new haircut, new clobber, a good lunch and a damn fine pint by the time you reach the end of the road. Twisted Lip is one of two micropubs on the street, offering a good selection of ales in its terraced house setting.

- **The Bottled Note**

  Up to a dozen rare drafts can be found at any given time at The Bottled Note on Borough Road. The pub, which morphs into a cocktail and wine bar at night, centres around a small, wood-panelled corner bar featuring cask and keg pumps from near and afar. Beers from the local Three Brothers Brewery in Stockton are usually in good supply. Make sure to try the Short and Stout if it's on.

Millwall

Fact box
Nickname – The Lions
Colours – Blue and white
Ground – The Den
Built in – 1993
Capacity – 20,146

Introduction

There was a time when drinking around Bermondsey before a Millwall fixture would have been ill-advised. Today it is practically mandatory. Since the advent of the craft beer revolution, the railway arches that occupy a mile-long stretch from London Bridge down to The Den have become home to many breweries that all showcase their wares in quaint taprooms serving a wide range of progressive and experimental styles. The Bermondsey Mile, as it has become known, is considered to be a Mecca for ale enthusiasts, and one of the most impressive stops drops you within a short walk of the ground.

What to eat and where to eat it

- **Manze's**

   A visit to Millwall is not complete without checking in with the godfather of pies at Manze's on Deptford High Street. The shop has been in the family for more than 100 years and still runs in much the same way as it did when it first opened. The pies are made by hand and served with fluffy mashed potatoes with parsley sauce (liquor) on top. For the real authentic experience, wash it down with a glass of hot or cold sarsaparilla, a traditional soft drink akin to root beer and produced to this day on Walworth Road in London by Baldwins.

- **Matchstick Piehouse**

   A slightly more modern version of the piehouse can be found in the Matchstick theatre, where a range of pies are chalked up alongside guest beers from the local breweries. Based in an industrial arts space, it has a rather eclectic feel which can be a bit hit and miss among football fans. But it is well worth seeking out for some good food and beer if you can bear the eclectic surroundings.

- **Express Fish Bar**

   If there is one thing that the end to a heavy day of craft ale exploration calls for, it is a round of tasty and plentiful fish and chips. Thankfully the Express Fish Bar provides this in spades, with fresh fish that spills over the edges of its oval plates and fluffy chips that lie invitingly by its side. The staff are always welcoming and there is plenty of space to sit down, relax and recall the day's events, depending on the quantity and strength of the beers consumed, of course.

What to drink and where to drink it

- **Fourpure Brewing Co. Basecamp**

  Beware of starting the day at Fourpure Brewing Co. Basecamp, because it's very difficult to leave. The newly renovated taproom is far more spacious and airy than most places on the Bermondsey Beer Mile and has two floors to enjoy beers from their horseshoe bar. The Easy Peeler, modelled on the vibrant coastal town of Cinque Terre, is a lovely, crisp, refreshing citrus session IPA well suited to a good booze up. Juicebox is equally delicious but slightly more potent.

- **London Beer Factory**

  Globally inspired but locally minded, the London Beer Factory is a craft brewery founded in early 2014 by brothers Ed and Sim Cotton. The duo have won acclaim since for their progressive style of brewing, which has created such wonders as a triple dry-hopped Triple IPA, and 'dusk' and 'dawn' wild ales. Their beers can be enjoyed in The Barrel Project, which serves house barrel-aged and craft beers.

- **Brew By Numbers**

  Brew By Numbers, or BBNo, is a stylish, chic brewery with a tasting room and taproom within a few doors of each other on Enid Street. Its beers are noticeable for their jet-black packaging, which often showcases a number to denote different experimentations. Beer number 01, a sloe and juniper gin-inspired saison, is well worth trying, as is their tropical interpretation of a Gose, found under number 19 on the shelf.

Milton Keynes Dons

Fact box
Nickname – The Dons
Colours – White
Ground – Stadium MK
Built in – 2007
Capacity – 30,500

Introduction

Milton Keynes. Satan's layby. Home to the grid system, code-cracking Bletchley Park, more roundabouts than any other town in the country and, if rumours are to be believed, even the elusive Illuminati. But if that isn't an impressive enough roll call, it is also home to a pizza franchise that put the 'two' in Tuesdays, the 'meat' in meatilicious and created a garlic and herb sauce that put the 'dip' in dipping. It is, of course, Domino's. Set up in 1960 by college dropout Tom Monaghan and his brother James, they opened their first store in Michigan under the name 'DomiNick's', which changed when Tom traded his Volkswagen Beetle for his brother's share of the business. The franchise model allowed them to rapidly expand and in 1985 they opened their first UK store in Luton. A former delivery driver at the store actually went on to own it and celebrated his 20th anniversary by opening his 23rd store and Domino's 1,100th in the UK. The so-called 'pizza tycoon' has seen the chain grow from tens of thousands of deliveries to hundreds of millions, largely thanks to central distribution points which use the latest technology to restock hundreds of outlets every second day. Quite fitting, therefore, that Milton Keynes is home to not only the Domino's HQ but also a behemoth warehouse supplying shops around the country – a home for pizza in the nation's roundabout capital.

What to eat and where to eat it

- **Bogota Coffee Company**

  They say that Colombia does three things well, but only one of them is legal. So if you get the chance, head down to the café named after the nation's capital to try some delicious coffee and tasty snacks; you won't be disappointed.

- **Domino's**

  You will encounter up to ten roundabouts on the walk from Milton Keynes Central to Stadium MK, and possibly many more if you drive in. But take comfort in the fact that you can find a perfectly good Domino's halfway between, with the headquarters right outside the ground.

- **Made in Sud**

  Check out the competition at Made in Sud, specialising in real Neapolitan pizza uncorrupted by American influence. Switch your 'American hot' for a 'salame Napule', your 'vegi supreme' for a 'vegana' and your 'absolute banger' for a delectable 'nduja pizza'.

What to drink and where to drink it

- **Brewhouse & Kitchen**

  Shiny copper beer tanks and salvaged industrial furnishings welcome you at one of Milton Keynes's premier beer destinations, the Brewhouse & Kitchen. A range of home-brewed keg and cask beers line the bar, with beer flight boards available for those who struggle with indecisiveness.

- **The Plough**

  Bedfordshire brewers since 1876, Charles Wells is part of the fabric in these parts, with hundreds of pubs stretching across the southern counties. Backing on to the canal, The Plough is a warm and cosy pub with a suntrap beer garden.

- **Cross Keys**

  A peaceful walk back from Stadium MK along the Grand Union Canal will bring you to the thatched roof and whitewashed walls of the Cross Keys, a country boozer just moments away from the modern grid system of Milton Keynes. Experience the town's former life as a rural village as you indulge in a pint of local beer.

Morecambe

Fact box
Nickname – The Shrimps
Colours – Red
Ground – Mazuma Stadium
Built in – 2009
Capacity – 6,476

Introduction

For hundreds of years, the channels, gutters and dykes of Morecambe Bay have provided locals with a plentiful supply of one of Britain's most-loved shellfish: shrimp. Traditionally fished using a hand net in shallow waters, the use of horses, tractors and eventually purpose-built boats called 'nobbies' were brought in to open up the bountiful catches that lay in the deeper channels. During the 1930s, the industry exploded as Morecambe Bay shrimp, delivered in neat little china pots, became popular on the fashionable tea tables of the London elite. Today only a handful of shrimp trawlers remain in the area manned by a dying breed of people with local knowledge of the shifting quicksand and tidal patterns of the area. But bolstered by programmes such as The Ark of Taste and Booths' Forgotten Foods project, which seek to protect endangered products, there could be a mini-revival in sight, with sales on the rise once again.

What to eat and where to eat it

- **The Lighthouse Café**

  No trip to Morecambe is complete without visiting the statue of the town's namesake celebrity, Eric, who stands in one of his characteristic poses with a pair of binoculars around his neck on the seafront. Across the street lies The Lighthouse Café, where you will find cakes, coffees and even a Knickerbocker Glory if that takes your fancy.

- **Edmondson's Fresh Fish**

  Sample the famous Morecambe Bay Potted Shrimps in their purest form at the renowned Edmondson's Fresh Fish shop, as featured by Rick Stein and Adrian Edmondson, among others. They trawl every day out in the bay, cooking the shrimp aboard their boat before taking them back to the shop for a second cook in creamy butter, salt and 'secret' spices, making the much-loved 'potted' flavour.

- **The Secret Bistro**

  Hidden amid the hustle and bustle of Morecambe's promenade, you will find one of the town's best restaurants in The Secret Bistro. The menu consists of British and European classic dishes served with a twist, such as 'nduja-spiced Scotch egg and Indian chicken Kiev, both notable picks. Find it above The Palatine pub, which is also an ideal spot for an aperitif.

What to drink and where to drink it

- **The Smugglers Den**

  Dating back to the early 17th century, The Smugglers Den is considered to be Morecambe's oldest pub, with a cavernous interior and (allegedly) a secret tunnel leading to the beach for the illicit transportation of goods. A pint in one of its many cosy snug areas is a fine way to enjoy a pre- or post-match drink.

- **The Little Bare**

  Get a taste of the north-west inside The Little Bare micropub on Princes Crescent. Local beers from breweries such as Fell, Westmoreland and Twisted Wheel line the bar, with cask and keg ales rotated regularly. In the father-and-son owners' words, it's a little space with a big choice.

- **Cross Bay Brewery**

  On the outskirts of town but within a half hour's walk of the Mazuma lies Cross Bay Brewery, a decade-old outfit with a charming oak-laden brewhouse. Premium, natural ingredients go into its deliciously moreish beers, with a fruity red IPA and an 'artistically made' Güell Mosaic the pick of the bunch. Those travelling up on the train, consider alighting at Lancaster on the West Coast Main Line, a short taxi ride away from the brewery.

Newcastle United

Fact box
Nickname – The Magpies
Colours – Black and white
Ground – St James' Park
Built in – 1892
Capacity – 52,305

Introduction

'Everything about the 1995/96 shirt was just perfect,' fan site *The Mag* wrote as it proclaimed the jersey the best version of Newcastle United's famed black and white stripes ever. Worn by club icons such as Les Ferdinand, Peter Beardsley and David Ginola, its baggy fit and effortlessly cool 'grandad collar' made it instantaneously iconic. At its heart was the Newcastle Brown Ale logo, with its famous Blue Star and silhouette of the Tyne Bridge. Brewed locally at the time, production moved to Gateshead in 2004 before moving to Tadcaster in North Yorkshire in 2010 when Scottish & Newcastle was bought out by Dutch brewing giants Heineken. But the Dog or Broon, as it is known locally, is still widely served in the city and its legacy is protected fiercely. Try asking for a pint glass with your bottle of Newkie Brown next time you are there to find out how.

What to eat and where to eat it

- **Pedalling Squares**

  The train ride into Newcastle tells you everything you need to know about the city's industrial past. Rows of terraced houses cut away as you duck under tunnels and over the high-level bridge, the juddering approach immortalised in the film *Get Carter*. A breakfast at Pedalling Squares in the once-famous iron-producing district of Swalwell is an excellent way to kick off the day, offering a rare and rather fashionable glimpse back in time.

- **Träkol**

  Housed in shipping units by the Tyne directly underneath the city's famous arch bridge is Träkol, a Scandinavian restaurant that derives its name from the Swedish word for charcoal. A focus on preservation, dry ageing and cooking over an open fire creates hearty dishes ranging from small plates to feasting options for two to share.

- **The Broad Chare**

  Expect well-kept beer, honest food and a hearty dose of the north-east at The Broad Chare, a traditional ale house on the Tyne banks. Enjoy 'middlewhite crackling with Bramley apple sauce' in the bar or a warm Scotch egg with a runny yolk centre. The dining room offers a wide range of classic British favourites in a comfortable loft setting.

What to drink and where to drink it

- **The Free Trade Inn**

  Transport yourself back to 1981 when The Free Trade Inn became the star of a national marketing campaign for Newcastle Brown Ale. Rowdy drinkers are filmed huddled around the bar sipping copious amounts of the Dog. As the camera pans out to reveal the docile Tyne in the background, the narrator questions, 'would the north-east really be as tranquil without it?'

- **The Tyne Bar**

  Head to the Ouseburn Valley for heritage, culture and a plethora of independent outlets that cluster around a small tributary of the River Tyne. At the bottom, you'll find The Tyne Bar sitting under the Ouseburn viaduct with a great selection of food and drink and a lovely beer garden to boot.

- **City Tavern**

  Find up to ten cask ales on rotation at any given time at the refined and sumptuous City Tavern pub on Northumberland Road. Its own house ales feature alongside guest beers from Wylam Brewery, Theakstons and even draught Newkie Brown.

Brighton & Hove Albion: *The Lanes shopping neighbourhood in Brighton, which helped elevate the city to the hipster capital of the world (Alamy)*

Bradford City: *An old Timothy Taylor-branded wagon rests at Oakworth Station on the Keighley & Worth Valley Railway (jackpeat)*

Brentford: *Griffin & Pride shire horses pulling the Fuller's Brewery dray, part of the historic brewery in Chiswick (Alamy)*

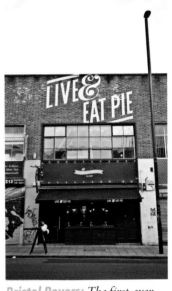

Bristol Rovers: The first-ever Pieminister restaurant in Stokes Croft, Bristol (courtesy of pieminister.co.uk)

Cheltenham: Cooper's Hill ahead of the Cheese-Rolling and Wake (Flickr)

Leeds United: The Old Peacock pub by Elland Road, where it is rumoured players would pop in for a pint at half-time back in the glory days (Wikimedia Commons)

Manchester City: The famous inflatable banana on show at the FA Cup semi-final in 2013, as Manchester City got their first taste of success (Alamy)

Millwall: *Manze's Pie Shop in Deptford, where you can get traditional pie, mash and liquor within walking distance of The Den in Millwall (jackpeat)*

Newcastle United: *The independent container community sitting beneath Tyne Bridge, as featured on bottles of Newcastle Brown Ale (jackpeat)*

Newport: *This Little Piggy sculpture by Sebastien Boyesen outside the Indoor Market, Newport, in South Wales (Alamy)*

Northampton Town: *The Brutalist Carlsberg Brewery in Northampton –
'probably' among the most striking breweries in the world (geograph.co.uk)*

Nottingham Forest: *The Nottingham cheese riot of 1766 (Working-Class
History)*

Oldham: A rag pudding served in an Oldham fish and chip shop (Wikimedia Commons)

Oxford United: Vaults and Garden café in Oxford, where you will find an excellent locally sourced Oxfordshire breakfast with a dollop of Oxford sauce on the side (Wikimedia Commons)

Plymouth Argyle: Cornish pasties in a shop window (geograph.co.uk)

Port Vale: The B'oatcake on the canal at Stoke-on-Trent selling oatcake, a North Staffordshire delicacy *(Alamy)*

Preston North End: The UK's first Kentucky Fried Chicken store in Preston, where a commemorative plaque remains today

Reading: Bel & The Dragon in an old biscuit factory in Reading *(jackpeat)*

Salford City: Eccles Old Thatched Cottage, Eccles cakes, early 1900s *(Alamy)*

Shrewsbury Town: *Interior view of Appleyards display in the historic town centre of Shrewsbury in Shropshire (Alamy)*

Southend United: *Cockles, mussels, shrimp and crayfish served with buttered bread in Leigh-on-Sea (jackpeat)*

Walsall: A traditional Black Country meal of faggots and chips served with a glass of beer (Alamy)

West Ham: Salmon salting at Forman & Field next to the London Stadium (jackpeat)

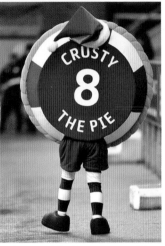

Wigan Athletic: Wigan Athletic mascot Crusty the Pie walks around the stadium wearing a festive hat before the beginning of the match (Alamy)

Wycombe Wanderers: The weighing of the mayor in Wycombe (geograph.co.uk)

Newport County

Introduction

Pork has been part of the Welsh diet since way back when. Mentioned in the 14th Century *Laws of Hywel Dda* by Howel the Good, the former king notes that 'out of the booty of swine he (the porter) is to have the sow which he can lift up by the bristles with one hand so that her feet shall be as high as his knees'. As a result, many families in the countryside would keep a pig which would be left to feed on waste ground and in woodlands until the time came to eat it with savoury Welsh cakes. Of course, not all pigs are destined straight for the plate. While some stay at home, others find their way to market, as is foretold in the toe-play nursery rhyme and depicted by Wales-based sculptor Sebastian Boyesen in his Newport-based statue *This Little Piggy*. To be found outside the town's Provisions Market, the Gloucester Old Spots pig is carrying baskets of fruit and vegetables and was erected to celebrate over 700 years of markets in Newport. Plans for a revamp of the market were given the go-ahead by the local council in 2020, with old stalls making way for a new workspace hub, offices and a food court and bar in the style of Cardiff's Tramshed.

What to eat and where to eat it

- **The Pot Café**

  Kick off the day in Newport's beautiful Victorian arcade at The Pot Café, a quaint continental-inspired bistro that offers a range of excellent breakfast options as well as several comforting home-cooked dishes for lunch.

- **Vacara's**

  A favourite among the locals, Vacara's fish shop dates back to the late 19th century, and not much has changed since then. Chip shop at the front, old-school restaurant at the back, you can expect the best of Welsh hospitality in this town-centre gem.

- **The Snug Restaurant & Café**

  Hidden away in the grounds of Newport's neighbouring Roman village, Caerleon, The Snug Restaurant & Café is worth going out of your way to experience. Pass through the Roman gate and its legionnaire guard at the entrance to the historic building.

What to drink and where to drink it

- **Tiny Rebel**

  Time was when only a handful of beer enthusiasts across Britain would have known about Tiny Rebel, a start-up microbrewing company based in Newport. Then Cwtch scooped Champion Beer of Britain in 2015 and all of a sudden the south Walian brewers became a mainstay in bars across the country. Find their brewery bar in the Wern Industrial Estate or a taproom just a stone's throw from the train station.

- **The Cellar Door**

  Find a host of independent cafés, restaurants and, most importantly, pubs on Clytha Park Road, a short walk from the train station. The Cellar Door is a micropub based in an old computer shop with no TV, games machines or pool table – just good, locally produced ales, ciders and the humdrum of jovial chitter-chatter.

- **Le Pub**

  Billed as a compact, buzzing bar and music venue hosting gigs by up-and-coming artists, Le Pub is an excellent place to wind down after the game with a good selection of beers on tap and an enticing cocktail list. Community-owned and not for profit, you will also find some delicious vegetarian and vegan food too.

Northampton Town

Fact box
Nickname – The Cobblers
Colours – Claret and white
Ground – Sixfields Stadium
Built in – 1994
Capacity – 7,798

Introduction

In April 2019, Danish multinational brewers Carlsberg were forced into an embarrassing admission. Contrary to a long-standing slogan and sizeable marketing efforts, they confessed they were probably *not* the best beer in the world and had instead become too preoccupied with 'being the biggest', a legacy they wished to undo by completely rebrewing the tipple 'from head to hop' and relaunching with a more 'honest' marketing campaign that would drive reappraisal. The new 'pilsner' would also do away with previous associations with 'beer' which came into being when the initial slogan was first dreamt up at the company's Brutalist brewery in Northampton on the banks of the River Nene. Inspired by a Danish longship, the building was awarded the *Financial Times*'s Industrial Architecture Prize in 1975 in recognition of its strong geometric form and a large glass gable end which exposes the tanks and pipes of the brewing equipment. It still stands today, and you might say it is among the most striking breweries in the world, probably.

What to eat and where to eat it

- **Giggling Sausage**

  Check out Carlsberg's home in the UK en route to the Giggling Sausage café, south of the River Nene. A good full English can be had at a reasonable price in the traditional greasy spoon.

- **The Good Loaf**

  When restaurant critic and MasterChef judge William Sitwell declared Northamptonshire Britain's 'most foodie county', he did so because, in part, it produces over 687 million loaves of bread a year. Sample a hearty range for yourself at The Good Loaf, where you will find sandwiches and paninis using locally sourced ingredients. The pastrami and Monterey Jack cheese come highly recommended.

- **Nuovo**

  Pick your way through the evening at Northampton's premier 'cicchetti' restaurant Nuovo, where carefully crafted and delectable-looking small Italian dishes crowd the table. Try a Moreta to kick things off, a traditional spritz made with Italicus Bergamot liqueur, Villa Ascenti dry gin and Prosecco.

What to drink and where to drink it

- **The Malt Shovel Tavern**

  Dressed in the style of a Belgian beer café, The Malt Shovel Tavern is a superb real ale pub located in the back garden of the Carlsberg brewery. Not that you will find much of 'the world's greatest' down here. Expect ales from Hook Norton, Oakham Ales and Phipps instead.

- **The Albion Brewery Bar**

  Find 'one of the finest pints of ale in the whole county' at The Albion Brewery Bar, according to its owners Phipps Brewery. Unlike Carlsberg, they may have a fair claim here, with a foaming session ale called Thrupenny, a moreish Cobblers and a rich Ratliffe's Stout worthy of such acclaim.

- **The Pomfret Arms**

  New on the Northampton scene, The Pomfret Arms is a spruced-up pub on the Nene banks offering home-brewed beers produced on-site in the Cotton End microbrewery. Along with its own, you will find ales from the award-winning Great Oakley Brewery in Tiffield, Siren, Tring, Framework and many more.

Norwich City

Fact box
Nickname – The Canaries
Colours – Yellow and green
Ground – Carrow Road
Built in – 1935
Capacity – 27,244

Introduction

Profiling a club that plies its trade in yellow and hails from a town famed for its mustard seemed too easy an introduction for a book like this, and indeed it was. Although Norwich City has long had close ties to Colman's, the colours actually originate from the canaries bred in the area after being introduced around the 16th century by a group of European immigrant weavers known as 'The Strangers'. The name was first used in records to mean anyone who was not a native of a particular town, and could well be applied to its Woking-born chairwoman and food personality Delia Smith. Along with her husband, Michael Wynn-Jones, she became a majority shareholder in 1996, steering the club to five promotions and suffering four relegations, the most noted of which was the turbulent '05 season when Smith took to the pitch during one game to rouse the fans. Her efforts were in vain, but that shouldn't stop you from borrowing her famed war cry on your next visit: 'Let's be 'havin you!'

What to eat and where to eat it

- **Olive's Café**

  Widely regarded as the best breakfast in Norwich, Olive's namesake brekkie is the stuff of legend in the local area, with a myriad of ingredients enticingly assorted on oversized plates that struggle to contain the bounty of food on offer. The café is housed in a traditional building just moments away from the quayside, making it an idyllic place to kick off the day.

- **Grosvenor Fish Bar**

  Dine like a pirate in Grosvenor's cavernous fish and chip 'grotto' on Lower Goat Lane. The hollowed-out basement provides space for 70 diners, with the exposed rock walls providing a unique backdrop to enjoy one of the 'best places to eat on a budget in the UK' according to *The Times*. And they fry in beef dripping, too!

- **Brummells**

  Find Norfolk coastal fare in a traditional 17th-century building at Brummells, a seafood restaurant and grill that harks back to a time gone by. Brancaster oysters are served in the half shell over ice, and local lobster is available in mornay or thermidor style. If you prefer something from the land, local Breckland wild deer venison steaks are prepared on the grill with a sweet and sour marsala and juniper berry jus.

What to drink and where to drink it

- **The Strangers Tavern**

  Named after the European settlers who landed in Norwich in the 16th century, The Strangers Tavern is a recently reopened pub in the heart of the city serving a range of local craft ales. Breweries from Norfolk, Suffolk and other nearby areas are well represented in the cosy bar area, where you'll also find a comprehensive range of wines and spirits.

- **Belgian Monk**

  Pay homage to Norwich's Flemish settlers at the Belgian Monk, a pub specialising in classic Belgian blondes as well as lesser-known beers from the continent. Modelled on the renowned beer-making monastery at Grimbergen, the Monk has exclusivity from four smaller regional Belgian breweries, allowing you to try something new. It also sells around 300 kilos of mussels a week, if you get peckish.

- **The Coach & Horses**

  Home to Chalk Hill Brewery, the longest-running independent brewery in Norwich, the Coach & Horses is a bustling local pub and brewhouse located a short walk away from the train station. A striking red, saloon-like exterior is sunken behind the terraced houses of Thorpe Road and oozes charm. Think Stuart Little's home, but grander and with more beer in it.

Nottingham Forest

Fact box
Nickname – Forest
Colours – Red
Ground – City Ground
Built in – 1898
Capacity – 30,445

Introduction

Nottinghamshire's distaste for the rich/poor divide has been well documented in literature thanks to its heroic outlaw who needs no Introduction, but in 1764 an uprising occurred that would have made even his Merry Men quake in their boots, such was the scale of the insurrection. That year's Goose Fair had got off to a typically jovial start as 20,000 fattened geese made the long walk to market from neighbouring counties, feet coated with tar and sand to protect them on their way. But the geese and the Michaelmas feast they would be sacrificed in celebration of had come to play second fiddle to the glorious cheese that would sit in resplendent wheels on stalls ready for feasting. At least, they were until the traders broke the bad news that prices had almost doubled and all hell broke loose. According to *The Date Book of Remarkable and Memorable Events Connected with Nottingham and its Neighbourhood*, 'the people were so exasperated that their violence broke loose like a torrent', with cheese being rolled down Wheeler Gate and Peck Lane at a chaotic rate. Even the mayor copped one as he tried to restore the peace, flattened by a

100lb wheel of dairy comeuppance, records note. It wasn't until cavalry and infantry units were deployed that peace was restored and the Nottingham cheese riot turned stale. And yet they chose to write books about a bloke in green tights. Go figure.

What to eat and where to eat it

- **The Loxley**

  South Yorkshire has gone some way in reclaiming Robin Hood of Loxley, even naming an airport after him. But it would be a crime not to humour Nottinghamshire's claim to the famed outlaw with an all-day pub breakfast at The Loxley, where you will find a good beer range too if you turn up at an agreeable hour.

- **The Mushy Pea Stall**

  Other than ducks and cheese, a modern-day staple at the Nottingham Goose Fair is mushy peas served with a big dollop of mint sauce. At any other time of year, The Mushy Pea Stall in the Victoria Market is the best place to stop to experience the time-honoured tradition.

- **The Cheese Shop**

  Discover whether the cheeses of Nottinghamshire and its surrounding counties are worth rioting over at The Cheese Shop, where you can experience a variety of locally sourced, British, artisanal produce. Just try not to quibble over the price.

What to drink and where to drink it

- **Trent Navigation Inn**

  Discover the Navigation Brewery range at the Trent Navigation Inn on the Notts County side of the river. An IPA, golden, pale and stout are regular features with the Smokin' Joe well worth a try if it is on, a dark smoked porter that will warm your cockles ahead of the game.

- **The Vat & Fiddle**

  Castle Rock's brewery tap, The Vat & Fiddle, is a 1930s art deco-style building beneath the iconic blue tower of the city brewery. You will find the full range across 13 hand-pulled taps, including Sherwood Reserve and Screech Owl.

- **Neon Raptor Brewing Company**

  The very definition of 'one for the road', the taproom at Neon Raptor Brewing Company showcases several punchy ales that will send you packing in style. A single-hopped Double New England IPA called Run Ekuanot Run comes in at a delicious eight per cent ABV, while the Hydra Fight sour is pushing ten per cent.

Oldham Athletic

Fact box
Nickname – Latics
Colours – Blue
Ground – Boundary Park
Built in – 1904
Capacity – 13,512

Introduction

In the days before ceramic basins, plastic boiling bags and other such cooking utensils, the people of Oldham came up with a more straightforward way of getting their savoury fill by wrapping delicious dollops of minced beef and onion gravy in a suet pastry that was contained within cotton or muslin cloths, creating the now-famous 'rag pudding'. Like many staple working-class meals that took root in the northern industrial heartlands, it was an easy way of making a little bit of meat go a long way, while filling up the hungry mill workers with lots of calories. Today they remain a common feature in chip shops, pubs and cafés around Oldham, with the Jacksons Farm Fayre factory pumping out an astonishing 800,000 of them a year. Owner Keith Jackson is responsible for the exponential growth, having left a successful job in the City to take over the wholesale butchery business from his dad. You could describe it as a real riches to rags story.

What to eat and where to eat it

- **Clean Plate Kitchen**

  Take up to 15 full English breakfast items for under a tenner at Clean Plate Kitchen, a popular self-contained dining spot just moments away from Oldham Central tram stop. Its whopping big fry-up comes with complimentary hot drinks or juices. You can't say fairer than that.

- **Jack Spratts**

  Widely considered to serve the best rag pudding in Oldham, Jack Spratts is a traditional chippy on the outskirts of town that dishes up the Lancashire staple with chips and lashings of gravy. Get off the tram at Hollinwood if you're making your way over from Manchester; there's a half-decent pub across the road if you get thirsty.

- **Smoke Yard**

  To be found in the heart of Oldham town centre in Parliament Square, Smoke Yard is a trendy restaurant serving meats from the grill and classic American kitchen comforts such as macaroni cheese and pork ribs. The hanging skewers are particularly good, especially paired with a choice of 'filthy fries'.

What to drink and where to drink it

- ## Cob and Coal

  Housing hundreds of businesses, Tommyfield Market Hall stands as the vibrant hub of local, independent traders in Oldham. At its heart is the Cob and Coal, a German-inspired micropub serving excellent real ales and regular Dunkel, Helles and Weissbier.

- ## The Bridge Inn

  Find beers from the JW Lees Greengate Brewery on tap at The Bridge Inn, with a number of experimental styles worth trying. If you have never drunk a lemon radler, champagne grisette or rhubarb and custard lactose IPA, this will be an experience.

- ## Ashton Arms

  A rotating wall of ales will welcome you in at the Ashton Arms, where local brews from Deeply Vale, Pictish and Joseph Holt hold regular spots. Traditional cider, perry and continental lagers can also be found in the fridge.

Oxford United

Fact box
Nickname – The U's
Colours – Yellow
Ground – Kassam Stadium
Built in – 1997
Capacity – 12,400

Introduction

'Great Britain is a historic sausage eating country,' the English Breakfast Society notes in its manual, *The English Breakfast Handbook*. With more than 400 varieties to choose from, we Brits put away millions of them every day in a whole host of dishes that use imaginatively coined names to denote their usage, including bangers and mash, toad in the hole and hot dogs in a bun (see *Derby County*). Yet amid a clamour for the more popular Lincolnshire (see *Lincoln City*) and Cumberland (see *Carlisle United*) sausages, we seem to have overlooked the more regional and, dare I say, more regal varieties that are increasingly falling out of favour on supermarket shelves. Manchester, for example, is home to a wonderful sausage that packs an earthy nutmeg and ginger taste, while Newmarket sausages are distinctly peppery in flavour. But perhaps one of my favourites is the Oxford sausage, which contains lemon, pork and veal for a slightly more refined taste. A favourite among the dons at Oxford University, it dates back to the 18th century and is also commonly referred to as the 'Oxfordshire skate'. It pairs very well with the spicy

Oxford sauce for those brave enough to try it. You will find a bottle down at David John's pie shop in the market or on the tabletops at Vaults & Garden.

What to eat and where to eat it

- **Vaults & Garden**

  There is only one thing that beats the Vaults & Garden's historic 14th-century backdrop in the heart of the University Church of St Mary the Virgin, and that is its locally sourced Oxfordshire breakfast with sausage, bacon, homemade baked beans and a good dollop of Oxford sauce on the side. The perfect way to start a day out in the famous university city.

- **David John Butchers**

  The biggest pie maker in Oxford can be found in the historic covered market in the city centre, which is well worth a visit on account of the architecture alone. Look out for a red stall with rows of steak and ale, chicken and ham, and pork pies peeking out from behind the windows.

- **Comie's Caribbean Grill**

  The best place to eat within walking distance of Oxford United's out-of-town Kassam Stadium, Comie's Caribbean Grill is an island-themed restaurant with a vibrant and feel-good atmosphere. Enjoy goat curry, jerk chicken and veggie food among colourful murals.

What to drink and where to drink it

- **The Library**

  Get in The Library and study some of Oxford's best beers in this quirky establishment on Cowley Road. Wedged between a row of shops and restaurants, the turquoise exterior gives the first impression of its relaxed, bohemian character. Beers from Loose Cannon get a regular showing, alongside an excellent national and international bottle and can selection.

- **Teardrop**

  Nothing washes down a David John's pie better than a craft ale from the nano pub and bottle shop, Teardrop, of the same market. Eclectic ales from Church Hanbrewery are in good stock alongside other small, local breweries whic take pride of place in this super stall.

- **Kings Arms**

  Within walking distance of the Kassam, the Kings Arms is a fantastic pub on the banks of the River Thames. Not to be confused with the King's Arms in the city centre, you will find a more rural and relaxed vibe here along with a good range of beers. It's the perfect place to warm up after being exposed to the elements in City's three-stand ground.

Peterborough United

Fact box
Nickname – The Posh
Colours – Blue
Ground – Weston Homes Stadium
Built in – 1913
Capacity – 15,314

Introduction

By modern means of transport, the journey from the village of Stilton on Peterborough's outskirts to Shoreditch in east London takes two hours on a good run, but more likely three with traffic. For most fans, this anecdotal observation is of little relevance, but it does help build the character profile of Cooper Thornhill, who is widely believed to have popularised the village's namesake cheese. For it was he who on 29 April 1745 rode that same journey both ways and then back again on horseback in 11 hours, 33 minutes and 52 seconds, thus winning a 500 guinea wager. Thornhill was the landlord of The Bell Inn and an enterprising chap who took advantage of the coaching inn's proximity to the Great North Road to sell local cheese to passing travellers making their way to and from London. As demand for the cheese grew, Thornhill struck a commercial agreement with renowned cheesemaker Frances Pawlett, who is thought to have produced the earliest standardised version of the blue-vein favourite. Today, it is widely known as one of Britain's quintessential cheeses, and you can sample it in all its glory in the still-standing Bell Inn, just off the modern-day A1.

What to eat and where to eat it

- **The Chalkboard**

  For people who are as fussy about their tea as I am, The Chalkboard's multicoloured brewing timers are a godsend and ensure that your first brew of the day is a good one. Enjoy it alongside a superb full English served with toast and Netherend Farm butter.

- **Tavan Restaurant**

  Indulge in mezzes and charcoal-grilled meats at one of Peterborough's most highly regarded eating spots on Lincoln Road. The Tavan Restaurant specialises in Moroccan and Turkish cuisine, serving up plates that are a feast for the eyes as well as the stomach.

- **The Bell Inn**

  Visit the place widely thought to have popularised Stilton cheese in the very village itself, a short drive out of Peterborough. The famous 'Stilton cheese sampler' is served with the chef's plum bread, celery chutney and grapes.

What to drink and where to drink it

- **The Stoneworks Bar**

  Based in one of the oldest buildings in Peterborough's Cathedral Square, The Stoneworks Bar is literally packed to the rafters with historic charm, featuring exposed brick and timeworn timber beams. It also has 23 keg lines, ciders and a shuffleboard.

- **Charters Bar**

  A real ale pub on the lower deck of a historic Dutch barge, Charters Bar is a regular haunt among football fans on matchdays, featuring around 500 guest ales a year. Moored on the River Nene, a short walk away from the Weston Homes Stadium, it is an ideal place for a drink on a Saturday afternoon, especially if the sun is out.

- **The Brewery Tap**

  Featuring an impossible-to-miss copper-still entrance, The Brewery Tap is an award-winning pub and microbrewery based in an old labour exchange. Featuring the full Oakham Ales range, you can pass many an hour working your way through its full range, with Thai food served if you get peckish.

Plymouth Argyle

Fact box
Nickname – The Pilgrims
Colours – Green
Ground – Home Park
Built in – 1892
Capacity – 18,600

Introduction

In 2006 Dr Todd Gray, chairman of the Friends of Devon's Archives, made a quite inflammatory claim. According to his research, the treasured Cornish pasty didn't originate from Cornwall at all but from Plymouth, in Devon, with references in financial records from 1510 predating the first known recipe published in 1746 by some 200 years. The discovery reignited long-standing tensions over the savoury treat that can be traced back over centuries, often relating to its proper composition which, it is claimed, gets tampered with more on the Cornish side. The cookbook *Cornish Recipes, Ancient and Modern* notes that the 'Devil never crossed the Tamar into Cornwall on account of the well-known habit of Cornish women of putting everything into a pasty'. Even he, they say, was 'not sufficiently courageous to risk such a fate'. But, alas, it was the Cornish version that in 2011 was given protected status by the European Commission, meaning that only pasties made within the county from a traditional recipe could carry the name. Since then, a 'genuine' pasty has been required to form the familiar 'D' shape, crimped on one side and filled with a chunky mixture of beef, swede, potato, onion and light seasoning, with no tampering allowed.

What to eat and where to eat it

- **Barbican Pasty Co.**
Home to the largest concentration of cobbled streets in Britain, the Barbican district is ideal for starting and ending a day in Plymouth's port city. Kick things off at the Barbican Pasty Co. with a good Cornish pasty or a wide range of other fillings, served inside a historic building with a lime green exterior which you cannot miss.

- **Ivor Dewdney**
Since 1935 the Ivor Dewdney pasty has been revered locally as one of the best the city has to offer. Filled with succulent beef and a secret blend of herbs and spices, this is a must-try for any visitors to Plymouth, with outlets in the city centre and close to the ground in Stoke Village.

- **The Original Pasty House**
Voted Plymouth's best pasty in 2017, The Original Pasty House is an ideal place to stop for provisions for the journey home. Options include spicy chicken and chorizo, Thai curry and a giant steak pasty.

What to drink and where to drink it

- **The Bread and Roses**
  Pine green walls, salvaged antiques and upcycled furniture
  fill the room at The Bread and Roses, a social enterprise
  pub in the heart of Plymouth. Expect local beers from
  Summerskills, Bays Brewery and Noss Beer Works.

- **The Plymouth Stable**
  Pizza, pies and cider await the weary traveller at The
  Plymouth Stable by the harbourside. It has more than 50
  varieties of cider on offer, from scrumpy to sweet, sparkling
  or still. Tasting boards and cider buckets are also available
  if you get struck by choice paralysis.

- **The Refectory Bar**
  Head back to the Barbican to visit the oldest working
  gin distillery in England at Plymouth Gin's Refectory Bar.
  Mixologists create some of the finest cocktails in the south-
  west with a gin that is still made in accordance with the
  original recipe from 1793.

Port Vale

Fact box
Nickname – The Valiants
Colours – White and black
Ground – Vale Park
Built in – 1950
Capacity – 19,052

Introduction

For Staffordshire lobby, see Stoke City
What is beige in colour, baked over high heat and historically mass-produced in Stoke? That's right, oatcakes. Known as 'Staffordshire oatcakes' to give them their full name or the 'Potteries Poppadom' to borrow the local moniker, the savoury delicacy dates back to the 18th century when it was the staple diet among local folk. Having to endure long, brutal winters, rather than wheat, the farmers grew oats, which would be cooked on a bakestone griddle and served with lard or cheese, much like a savoury crêpe. They are no less popular today, with dozens of shops in the city still saving the local delicacy. Grab one for breakfast with sausage, bacon and eggs wrapped up with melted cheese in the middle.

What to eat and where to eat it

- **High Lane Oatcakes**

  Give yourself a famous Potteries welcome with breakfast at High Lane Oatcakes, where a sausage, egg and cheese oatcake wrap will make you glad you made the journey. You can also buy a dozen oatcakes for the road for under £3, perfect for smuggling into the game.

- **JB Oatcake Bakery**

  Watch the oatcake process unfold in front of your eyes at JB Oatcake Bakery, where rows of flatbreads are cooked and cooled in a homogenous and therapeutic style behind the counter. The bakery also makes thin crumpets called pikelets which are best served with jam or just butter.

- **The Slamwich Club**

  Inspired by a love of sandwiches, music and good times, The Slamwich Club is the brainchild of Stoke born and 'bread' best friends Nicole and Steph. Using only locally baked bread and the best ingredients, their sandwiches are a step up from anything else. Try their 'chimmi chimmi bang bang' if you want proof – sliced rump steak served with chorizo, Manchego cheese and, of course, chimichurri sauce.

What to drink and where to drink it

- **The Bulls Head**

Sample local beer from brewing behemoth Titanic at its first pub in Burslem, The Bulls Head. Up to ten real ales can be found on the bar at any one time, with cosy carpeted rooms creating a welcoming environment. The pub also puts on a barbecue on for all Port Vale's home games.

- **The Holy Inadequate**

Spectacular pub name aside, The Holy Inadequate is also one of the best pubs in Stoke-on-Trent. Traditional, snug and stocked up to the nines with good ales and snacks, you will feel right at home here. Be sure to try one of its delicious pork pies with your beer.

- **BottleCraft**

Curators of the best local and national ales, BottleCraft is an intimate bottle shop and bar that stocks 150 bottles, cans, and ten keg and two cask beers. Take a pew by the bar or head upstairs, where there is a small, intimate seating area.

Portsmouth

Fact box
Nickname – Pompey
Colours – Blue
Ground – Fratton Park
Built in – 1899
Capacity – 20,620

Introduction

At the end of the 19th century, the founding directors of Portsmouth FC created a ruse. Rather than name their newly built football ground after the borough of Milton to which it truly belonged, they decided to call it Fratton Park to disingenuously trick supporters into thinking it was within walking distance of Fratton railway station. Anyone who has visited the stadium on a matchday will attest that the ploy most definitely worked and, as far as the pages of this book are concerned, we should be thankful that it did. For alongside the station one of the other distinguishable aspects of Fratton is its high proliferation of greasy spoon cafés, which are more numerous than in most other commercial outposts. The term, which has become synonymous with cafés specialising in fry-up breakfasts served on tables lined with glass sugar dispensers and squeezy sauce bottles, actually dates back to at least the mid-19th century, when the first recorded usage appears in Samuel Bevan's *Sand and Canvas*. In it, he recalls a café in Rome 'so murky and so very far removed from cleanliness that the Germans have bestowed upon it the appellation of the "Dirty Spoon"', a term adopted henceforth for cafés specialising in fried or grilled foods. Thankfully that is just what one wants ahead of an away day on the south coast, and whether it be 2 Nice, Chit Chats, Bridge or The Fratton itself, many will be happy to oblige within walking distance of that dastardly train station.

What to eat and where to eat it

- **The Fratton**

  The pick of Fratton's greasy spoons is its namesake café, which presides less than a five-minute walk from the train station. Choose from breakfast 'sets' printed across laminated menus. The 'Fratton special' has an undeniable appeal, consisting of the full works with black pudding and bubble to boot.

- **Arepa 2GO**

  Head to the Outside-In Food Court in a hidden warehouse in the centre of Portsmouth for some of the best food choices the city has to offer (outside of greasy cafs). Venezuelan 'arepas' can be found at the fantastic Arepa 2GO stall. Think bao buns stuffed with burrito fillings.

- **Huis**

  Finish the day eating moules-frites and sipping a La Chouffe Blonde at Huis, an independent eatery marrying Belgian beer and food culture. Decorated in a typical continental style, you will find up to 100 beers waiting to be freed from its impressive beer cage, along with an extensive menu that includes traditional Belgian dishes cooked in beer.

What to drink and where to drink it

- **Staggeringly Good Brewery**
  With the old, rusty floodlights of Fratton Park looming in the distance, the Staggeringly Good Brewery is the perfect place to kick off an away day in Portsmouth. Serving a range of experimental beers in the world's first 'dinosaur church' taproom, you will find what it lacks in modesty it makes up for in intrigue.

- **The Froddington Arms**
  Before Fratton Park there was Fratton, and before Fratton there was Froddington, a Saxon name which originally meant 'Frodda's farm' or 'Frodda's village'. You will find a pub on Fratton Road still named after the original, with beers from Ringwood Brewery commonly on tap.

- **The Brewers Tap**
  Find the fantastic full range of Southsea Brewing Co. beers on tap in a small and vibrant pub on Eastney Road. Up to 14 craft ales are commonly on at The Brewers Tap, all of which are beamed on to the wall behind the beer lines. The perfect pit stop before the long journey home.

Preston North End

Fact box
Nickname – The Lilywhites
Colours – White
Ground – Deepdale
Built in – 1875
Capacity – 23,404

Introduction

Fast food has no place on these pages, yet it would be remiss not to recognise one of the first-ever outlets to grace our streets on Fishergate in Preston. Back in 1965, Ray Allen opened the UK's first Kentucky Fried Chicken store after meeting Colonel Harland Sanders himself two years earlier. The arrival came almost a decade before McDonald's, Burger King and Pizza Hut and is commemorated with a plaque in the shop. Today KFC has more than 900 branches in the UK and five in the wider Preston area. Those familiar with the opening more than 50 years ago say the Colonel was on hand to personally pick the first waiters and waitresses who worked there, although it is not known whether he indulged in some of the local delicacies such as Lancashire hotpot, Chorley cakes and butter pie while in the north-west.

What to eat and where to eat it

- **Brew + Bake**

  Housed under a contemporary glass and timber-clad structure, Preston's urban market cuts an impressive figure in the heart of the city, offering an abundance of fresh and local produce as well as top cafés and independent shops. Reminiscent of Copenhagen's Torvehallerne and Madrid's Mercado de San Miguel, the warm indoor setting is best enjoyed in the hands of Brew + Bake, where you'll find good coffee and famous fry-ups.

- **Deans Bakery**

  A fresh-baked smell and a glass counter of savoury treats will draw you into Deans Bakery, where you can sample Lancashire's famous butter pie, among other things. Dating back to the days when the predominantly Catholic population would abstain from meat on Fridays, the pie contains thinly sliced potato, onions, butter and sometimes a pinch of black pepper, all encased in pastry. Eat with a side of pickled red cabbage if you can get your hands on some.

- **KFC, Fishergate**

  Visit the UK's first Kentucky Fried Chicken on Fishergate, where a plaque commemorates Ray Allen and Colonel Harland Sanders' historic agreement to bring the southern fried chain to British shores. According to folklore Allen, who sadly died in 2019, had a handwritten copy of the Colonel's secret recipe, although he didn't care for it much himself.

What to drink and where to drink it

- **Black Horse**

Packed to the rafters with history and charm, the Black Horse is a must-visit pub for any travelling fan, showcasing ornate furnishings, mosaic floors and a bar with an expressive tiled curvature. It serves mainly Robinsons beers, including Unicorn, Old Tom and Dizzy Blonde.

- **Winckley Street Ale House**

Find up to ten keg and four cask beers chalked up at the Ale House on the cobblestoned Winckley Street. Formerly the Otter's Pocket, the single-room boozer has an intimate feel to it. Along with a wide range of beers, it also has a good menu of traditional pub food, including the legendary butter pie.

- **Plau Gin & Beer House**

Step back in time at the Plau Gin & Beer House, which dates back to 1668 and still retains much of its original characteristics. Recently transformed during a three-year renovation project which uncovered secret rooms and hidden histories, the bar is now a working museum serving many of our beloved modern treats.

Queens Park Rangers

Introduction

Every year across two days of the August Bank Holiday, come rain or shine, London's West End becomes a tapestry of vibrant colour, incredible aromas and pumping sound as the British West Indian community put on the ultimate celebration of cultural pride in the face of oppression and discrimination. The Notting Hill Carnival, hosted on the doorstep of Queens Park Rangers' home ground Loftus Road, dates back to the mid-1900s when Rhaune Laslett decided to hold a week-long festival to celebrate the cultural richness of the area in response to recent race riots. Held in the manner of a traditional British fête, the festival included pageants, food stalls and live music to begin with, but when Russell Henderson and his Trinidadian steel band turned up to find they were playing alongside a donkey cart and a clown, he decided it was high time to 'make this thing come alive'. So he started by walking the band up and down the street, then went a little further, then a bit further still, until more and more people would start peeling away from their shopping to join in. Speaking to *The Guardian* shortly before his death in 2015, Henderson noted that 'there was no route,

226

really – if you saw a bus coming, you just went another way'. The familiar ring of steel percussion still sounds out to this day, when millions of people descend on west London for the carnival, complemented by the smell of jerk pits cooking up Jamaican-style chicken as well as Trinidadian 'roti' and Guyanese 'pepper pot'. Most of the culinary specialities exist in good supply all year round in an area of London that now proudly celebrates its diverse ethnic make-up.

What to eat and where to eat it

- **Wild Thyme Café**

  If you arrive in west London feeling Hank Marvin (starving), then a good, family-run Colonel Gaddafi (café) is what you will need. For a slightly more upmarket vibe, head to the Wild Thyme Café near Loftus Road, where you will find a good fry-up and an even better Bloody Mary.

- **Chicken Kitchen**

  The world is your oyster at Goldhawk Road's Chicken Kitchen, where you can grill it, fry it or jerk it depending on your preference. Get your fill alongside an order of rice 'n' peas, 'Mommy's special coleslaw' or fried plantain.

- **Cottons**

  Half an hour sitting at Cottons' famous rum bar will be enough to warm your cockles following a long afternoon on the terraces. The Caribbean restaurant holds the Guinness World Record for the highest number of rums commercially available – 372 to be precise – helping you celebrate carnival-style all year long. You will also find a delightful array of food options, including wings, jerk chicken, pork and curried mutton.

What to drink and where to drink it

- **The Crown & Sceptre**

  Start the day's drinking with a pint of London Pride from the local Fuller's brewery (see *Brentford*). The Crown & Sceptre is a traditional Shepherd's Bush pub with ornate wooden furnishings and a small beer garden.

- **Defectors Weld**

  Leather chairs, hanging lights and exposed brick walls are on show at the Defectors Weld, an old pub with a modern twist on Shepherd's Bush Green. There are typically five rotating real ales chalked up next to the bar alongside some of London's best craft beer producers such as Beavertown, Five Points, Camden and Brixton.

- **The Distillery**

  Finish the day with a Portobello Road gin at The Distillery bar in Notting Hill. The striking blue exterior gives way to the ground floor Resting Room bar and Malt Floor cocktail lounge upstairs. A good selection of locally sourced, seasonal small plates is also available for grazing.

Reading

Introduction

Up until the 19th century, Reading didn't have too much to shout about on the culinary front. Other than its eponymous Cocks's Sauce with the familiar bright orange branding, which preceded Yorkshire Relish and Worcester sauce, it had faded from the food scene. That was, at least, until Joseph Huntley arrived, soon to be joined by his cousin George Palmer, and started to produce some of the best biscuits on the market. Relaxed corn duties allowed the pair to ramp up production until by the early 20th century their biscuit factory employed thousands of people and spanned some 24 acres across Reading, with shipments of the iconic Huntley & Palmers biscuit tins going to remote parts of Asia, Africa, America and beyond. Today the town's biscuit heritage is marked in the borough's Three Bs slogan – biscuits, bulbs and beer – with the latter a nod to William Blackall Simonds' brewing ventures, which at one point produced just over one per cent of all the beer brewed in the country. Reading FC, more commonly known as the Royals these days, were also known as The Biscuit Men for many years and, as far as these pages are concerned, will continue to be so.

What to eat and where to eat it

- **Café YOLK**

  Purveyors of a 'legendary' breakfast, Café YOLK offers everything you could want and more in a social setting a short walk away from Reading train station. A cross between an American breakfast diner and an English café, you won't be short of options with pancakes, waffles and, unsurprisingly, lots of eggs on the menu.

- **Shed**

  For sourdough toasties, doorstop sandwiches, stuffed wraps and no-nonsense Italian coffee, head to family-run Shed in an old forge by the train station. Try its 'Terry vegan' range or indulge in a classic chicken sandwich. The outlet even does a crisp butty if that takes your fancy, served with mature cheddar, mayo, French's mustard and tomato.

- **Bel & The Dragon**

  A former biscuit factory located on the Kennet & Avon Canal waterfront, Bel & The Dragon is a charming restaurant that retains many features of its former self. Classic, upmarket British dishes and roasted meats account for most menu options. Try the fantastic vanilla panna cotta with port jelly and ginger biscuits for dessert.

What to drink and where to drink it

- **Double-Barrelled Brewery**

  Boasting a dozen lines of draught beer, the taproom at Double-Barrelled Brewery is a fine place to kick off a day in Reading. Named after co-founders Mike and Luci Clayton-Jones, who first brewed their Double-Barrelled beer as favours on their wedding day, you will find a generous range of beers to enjoy in their airy industrial unit. Try the Parka and the Ding as an introduction.

- **Hop Leaf**

  Home to Reading's only bar billiards table, this wet-led boozer prides itself on being a drinkers' pub with a no-nonsense attitude to getting you good beer in an unfussy setting. According to the website shitandnotshitpubsinreading.com, you will find 'nice booze and friendly people' at prices you can afford.

- **The Weather Station**

  A craft beer pub in the true sense of the word, The Weather Station is packed to the rafters with experiential beer styles, beanie hats and bushy beards. Expect hoppy IPAs, double IPAs, triple IPAs and numerous other left-field styles at this hipster paradise.

Rochdale

> **Fact box**
> Nickname – The Dale
> Colours – Blue
> Ground – Spotland Stadium
> Built in – 1878
> Capacity – 10,249

Introduction

Capitalism has given rise to skyscrapers in America, sprawling desert metropolises in the Middle East and sushi on conveyor belts in Asia, but it first trembled on the cobblestone streets of Rochdale when the Society of Equitable Pioneers was born in 1844. As the mechanisation of the Industrial Revolution put more people out of work and increased the rate of poverty, a group of tradesmen decided to band together to open a store selling food items many people couldn't otherwise afford. They designed the now-famous Rochdale Principles, which provided the basis of the modern cooperative movement, opening a store with essentials such as butter, oatmeal and candles before expanding their selection to include tea and tobacco. They were soon known for providing high-quality, unadulterated goods, uncommon at a time when many other traders would sell flour with chalk mixed in or tea bulked out with hedge clippings. Today you can visit the Rochdale Pioneers Museum to learn more about its origins, with a rather delightful pub annexed on its side.

What to eat and where to eat it

- **The Medicine Tap**

  Coffee house, cookhouse, bar and beer house rolled into one, The Medicine Tap is a dream first stop on any away day. Ribble Valley sausages, black pudding, hash browns and a toasted bloomer make up their 'mighty full tap breakfast' and can also be served in a flatbread or bap if you prefer. But if you go for the breakfast, stay for the real ale selection – a few pre-game tonics here are a must.

- **Wilbutts Lane Chippy**

  Less than 20 yards separate Wilbutts Lane Chippy from the terraces of Spotland Stadium. Situated at the end of a row of terraced houses, the shop occupies an old front room and quickly gets busy on matchdays. You can also try a local delicacy, rag pudding. Suet pastry encases minced meat and onions which spill generously over your chips.

- **Bombay Brew**

  Marrying Indian street food and craft ale, Bombay Brew is the ultimate post-match stop providing an ample, ever-changing menu of small dishes that pair perfectly with a range of inventive beers. Head to the lounge by the fireplace when you arrive for a beer and an appetiser before moving to more spacious surrounds for the main meal.

What to drink and where to drink it

- **The Baum**
  Located on the old cobblestoned streets of Rochdale's heritage area next door to the Pioneers Museum is The Baum, a pub befitting its historical setting. Old marketing boards for Fry's Chocolate and Irlam's Tripe adorn the building's front, with a wood-panelled interior showcasing several other exciting artefacts inside. Expect beers from Vocation, Track and the local Pictish Brewery on tap.

- **The Old Post Office Ale House**
  You will find the best selection of local ales one stop before Rochdale in Castleton, a three-minute train journey from town or a short drive straight to the ground. The Old Post Office Ale House might be small and unassuming, but it punches above its weight on the ale front with an impressive selection from across Lancashire and beyond.

- **Cemetery Hotel**
  Known locally as The Cem, this typical Lancastrian boozer has remained largely unchanged since Edwardian times and looks and feels all the better for it. A short walk away from Spotland Stadium, it is the perfect place to enjoy a pre- or post-match ale.

Rotherham United

Fact box
Nickname – The Millers
Colours – Red
Ground – New York Stadium
Built in – 2012
Capacity – 12,021

Introduction

In 2008 popular TV chef Jamie Oliver set out on a mission: to make Rotherham 'the culinary capital of the United Kingdom'. Establishing the country's first Ministry of Food since the Second World War, he hoped that a 'pass it on' scheme would create a town full of chefs out of people who, in his words, are used to 'eating out of styrofoam boxes seven days a week'. Trouble was, he wasn't popular in the area to begin with. In 2006 parents of schoolchildren, unhappy at the 'overpriced low-fat rubbish' that was served up as part of the *Jamie's School Dinners* campaign, launched a 'meals on wheels service' to school gates offering fish and chips, hamburgers and fizzy drinks. Such opposition would prove too much to overcome in the end, with Jamie's Ministry boarded up in 2017 amid an explosion of fast-food outlets which had doubled in number since the social enterprise was founded. But it wasn't all for nothing. Since the project opened, it claims to have shown more than 10,000 people how to cook, many of whom will have 'passed it on' since, while at Rawmarsh School the number of students eating healthy dinners has increased markedly.

The culinary revolution may never have materialised, but there's no doubting the Naked Chef left a lasting legacy and made a genuine, positive contribution to the well-being of Rotherhamites.

What to eat and where to eat it

- **Fitzwilliam & Hughes**
A short walk over the River Don from the train station will bring you to the historic Rotherham Minster and gardens, where the adjacent Fitzwilliam & Hughes has been selling good-quality coffee and cakes for generations. Stop off for a good bacon sandwich on arrival, or porridge oats if you want to be healthy.

- **Miele Delicatessen**
Purveyors of fine continental cheese and salamis, Miele Delicatessen is an ideal place to stop for a spot of pre-game lunch in Rotherham. Buckets of olives and chunky cured meats are kept behind a glass counter next to a seemingly endless selection of cheeses from across Italy and beyond.

- **Forward to Ethiopia**
An award-winning eatery in the heart of Rotherham offering 100 per cent vegan Ethiopian and Jamaican food, this is the sort of place that would make Jamie Oliver beam with pride. Chickpea curry, ital stew and a fabulous 'Rastafari special' are among the health-centric menu options, along with a range of wraps and juices.

What to drink and where to drink it

- **Cutlers' Arms**

  Grab a pint of Mighty Millers or New York Pale at Cutlers' Arms courtesy of local brewers Chantry. You will also find a selection of Belgian beers in this pub with views over the New York Stadium.

- **New York Tavern**

  Another Chantry pub within a short walk of the stadium, the New York Tavern is a corner pub with at least half a dozen cask ales on at any one time. Locally consumed snuff from Wilsons of Sharrow is also usually on sale in cherry, menthol or fruit flavours.

- **The Golden Ball**

  With a rustic log cabin-like interior and roaring coal fires, The Golden Ball is the perfect spot to unwind post-game and warm the cockles over a pint of ale and good food. Located in the charming village of Whiston, you will find it is worth making the journey for if time allows.

Salford City

Fact box
Nickname – The Ammies
Colours – Red
Ground – Moor Lane
Built in – 1978
Capacity – 5,108

Introduction

Rivalries aren't uncommon in this part of the world, but few are as fierce as the feud between two of the Eccles cake's earliest purveyors, James Birch and James Bradburn. Spotting a market for the sweet treat, a flaky pastry filled with dried currants, candied lemon, orange zest, sugar and spices, Birch opened a shop opposite Eccles Parish Church in 1796 and was soon in a position to upscale, moving to larger premises across the road. To avoid confusion, he erected a sign that read 'Eccles Cake Makers Removed from Across the Way' on the building, which still stands today. But when he moved, Bradburn, a former employee of his, had the shop rebuilt and installed a sign which certainly didn't sugarcoat his intentions, if you'll excuse the pun. 'Original and Oldest Established Eccles Cake Shop, Never Removed,' it read, and so the feud began. Today there is only one prominent bakery still producing the cakes in Eccles, run by the Edmonds family since the 1930s. But even they are not without their rivalries. In 2004 Greggs decided to drop the cakes from all its 1,200 shops, including the branch on the same street on which Birch first peddled his wares at the end of the 18th century. Talk about being caster-side.

What to eat and where to eat it

- **The Treehouse**

  Find the best breakfast this side of Manchester at The Treehouse café, where sweet and savoury treats can be enjoyed among the tastefully upcycled decor. If your trip precedes a few pre-match ales, then be sure to order the breakfast burger, which will set you up for the day. A thick rasher of bacon, sausage, spinach, black pudding and eggs are served in a brioche bun with a big dollop of hollandaise sauce.

- **Ward's Bakery**

  As the last remaining bakery in Eccles that makes its namesake cakes on-site, Ward's Bakery has become a proud champion of the local delicacy, particularly in the battle against high street adversaries. When Greggs announced it would be pulling the cake from its shelves, councillor Eddie Sheehy took 60 of them to an assembly of Salford representatives in solidarity with the cake, and they were all duly scoffed with a cup of tea before business started.

- **The Rivals Bar and Restaurant**

  Enjoy the best of British within the relaxed and welcoming architecture of the Royal Exchange's Great Hall, just a short walk from Salford Central station. Tables with red chequered cloths occupy its indoor beer garden, with a dining menu that includes the famous Eccles cake and Lancashire cheese combo on certain days.

What to drink and where to drink it

- **Seven Bro7hers**

  Tuck into Seven Bro7hers beers and a good selection from other local breweries at this taproom where you can enjoy watermelon wheat beer and session craft beer straight from the tank, as well as a smoked porter from Runaway Brewery and flat white stout from Alphabet Brewing.

- **The Kings Arms**

  Dating back to 1807, when Bloom Street was bustling with shops, people and plenty of beer houses to keep them well watered, The Kings Arms remains a proud part of the Salford community, regularly hosting societies, art exhibitions, fringe festivals and gigs. Six handpumps provide a good selection of bitters, stouts, milds, golden ales and even ultra-pale ales.

- **Ashley Brook**

  With links to the historic Joseph Holt Brewery, you will get the full range of cask, keg and bottled beers at the Ashley Brook, named after the shallow stream that once ran beneath it. The Crystal Lager is a popular choice among locals, but you might want to try the Manchester Brown for something a little different.

Scunthorpe United

Fact box
Nickname – The Iron
Colours – Claret and blue
Ground – Glanford Park
Built in – 1987
Capacity – 9,088

Introduction

With hundreds of square miles of naturally flat plains of low-lying land, canals, windmills, hordes of cyclists and cheese encased in colourful wax jackets, you could be forgiven for thinking you have arrived in the Netherlands as the train rolls over the River Trent and into Scunthorpe. At one point, around 800 windmills were grinding flour for the county's inhabitants, only a few hundred shy of those in operation across the North Sea. But while the Netherlands has worked hard to keep its windmills in at least partial working order, winds of change in Lincolnshire have left many of its mills in ruins, and there are only a handful left. Thankfully one notable exception exists in Scunthorpe, where a former mill has been converted into a rather lovely fine dining experience. Make sure to also look out for Cote Hill's Yellowbelly cheese which showcases a mild taste with a subtle tang. Matured in a yellow wax jacket, it will take you straight back to the streets of Amsterdam and the many rolls of Gouda, Edam and Maasdam cheeses that can be spotted piled in shop windows, usually next to a bike or two.

What to eat and where to eat it

- **Jennifer's Coffee Lounge**

  For home-cooked and honest food, start the day off in the hands of Jennifer, who cooks up a killer breakfast sandwich and serves a mean cup of tea. Make sure to stuff a sausage roll in your pocket on the way out, made with Lincolnshire sausage meat from a local butcher.

- **Klumpe**

  Kick back with a Butautu beer and hearty servings of herring, smoked pig ears and 'Mum's zeppelins' at Scunthorpe's sole Eastern European restaurant, Klumpe. Literally translated as 'wooden shoe', the small eatery displays a pair of clogs outside in a (most likely accidental) nod to the town's Dutch similarities.

- **San Pietro**

  Visit one of the few remaining windmills in Lincolnshire at San Pietro, a converted bed and breakfast and Italian fine dining restaurant. Reflecting the owner's Sicilian heritage, you can expect to find freshly made pasta, meat and fish dishes along with several delightful fine wines.

What to drink and where to drink it

- **Take a Gander**

  Those heading to the game by train might consider stopping off at Althorpe, where the fascinating Keadby Bridge welcomes you into the home of steel. The Take a Gander pub is a short stroll away on the River Trent banks and is within walking distance of Glanford Park if you happen to lose track of time.

- **The Honest Lawyer**

  Beers from Milestone, Great Newsome and Lincolnshire breweries make regular appearances on tap at The Honest Lawyer pub in the heart of Scunthorpe. A long ground-floor bar sits beneath a restaurant that serves decent grub if you get a bit peckish.

- **The Penny Bank**

  Finish the day with some live music in The Penny Bank pub, where a spacious bar area provides ample room for punters to strut their stuff well into the night. Draught beers from Batemans of Skegness are also commonly on the bar, including Prohibition craft lager.

Sheffield United

> **Fact box**
> Nickname – The Blades
> Colours – Red and white
> Ground – Bramall Lane
> Built in – 1855
> Capacity – 32,050

Introduction

Fan anthems hold a special place in Association football culture. 'You'll Never Walk Alone' is synonymous with Liverpool and Celtic, while 'Blue Moon' (Manchester City), 'I'm Forever Blowing Bubbles' (West Ham) and 'No one likes us, we don't care' (Millwall) are commonly bellowed out at home games in their respective stadiums. However, at Bramall Lane, supporters chose to adapt rather than adopt a cult song, skinning the lyrics to 'Annie's Song' by John Denver to give it a regional twist. Referencing the small pleasures one can enjoy in the Steel City, it cites Yorkshire-brewed Magnet bitter from John Smith's, Woodbine cigarettes and snuff tobacco, along with the eponymous chip-shop sandwich from which it takes its name. It is one of the few songs that can double up as an away guide for a day out in Yorkshire, so without further ado, let the 'Greasy Chip Butty Song' lead your way:

> *You fill up my senses, Like a gallon of Magnet,*
> *Like a packet of Woodbines, Like a good pinch of*
> *snuff, Like a night out in Sheffield, Like a greasy*

chip butty, Like Sheffield United, Come thrill me
again. Na na na na na ... Ooooohh!

What to eat and where to eat it

- **Tamper Sellers Wheel**
  Bringing New Zealand café culture to Sheffield, the Tamper
  Sellers Wheel combines speciality bakes from local Depot
  Bakery and wonderfully aromatic barista-served coffee to
  create a superb breakfast spot in an industrial backdrop.
  On the food front, the mince on toast is well worth a try,
  consisting of braised beef shin on toasted ciabatta with a
  poached egg and fresh hollandaise on top.

- **Brenda's Fish & Chips**
  A proper chippy in the heart of Sheffield, Brenda's is the
  best place to head for a greasy chip butty, in accordance
  with the popular matchday song. Order with scraps and a
  mug of tea for the whole experience.

- **Man Friday**
  Chances are that you will hear the lyrics of 'The Greasy
  Chip Butty Song' being belted out while you wait for your
  order at Man Friday chip shop, located behind the Kop end
  of Bramall Lane. Expect long queues as this is a popular
  haunt for home fans.

What to drink and where to drink it

- **Sheffield Tap**
  Step off the train and into the Sheffield Tap, one of the best station pubs in Yorkshire, which is high praise indeed in a county where good railway pubs are ten a penny. Housed in an old first-class refreshment room dating back to 1904, there is now a generous seating area, ample selection of real and craft ales and an on-site microbrewery.

- **Jabbarwocky**
  Beers from the Brewery of Saint Mars of the Desert, Thornbridge and Brew York can be found at the innovatively named Jabbarwocky pub in Highfield. Homemade dumplings with potato, bacon and cheese fillings also pair surprisingly well with their carefully curated list of beers.

- **Sheaf View**
  Enjoy a smooth pint of Neepsend Blonde on sunny days or a Renaissance red from Geeves in the winter months at the Sheaf View. Other local pubs, The Blake and The Wellington, are run by the same company and are well worth checking out if you have time.

Sheffield Wednesday

```
Fact box
Nickname – The Owls
Colours – White and blue
Ground – Hillsborough Stadium
Built in – 1899
Capacity – 39,732
```

Introduction

In 1899 a salesperson from a little-known confectionery brand in Sheffield called Bassett's accidentally made the discovery of a lifetime. Visiting a customer in Leicester, he knocked a tray of his samples on to the floor, scattering them everywhere. As he started to gather them up, the buyer took an interest in the oddly shaped sweets and placed an order there and then, asking if Bassett's would supply him with 'all sorts mixed together'. The new-found assortment proved an instant hit and allowed the company to expand into larger premises in Sheffield's Owlerton district, where it remains today, a short paddle from Hillsborough on the River Don. The company's mascot, Bertie Bassett, is made up of liquorice allsort pieces and has been a prominent feature in the branding since the 1920s. In 2009 he was 'married' off to Betty Bassett at the company's factory by a vicar who was aptly called Reverend Sweetlove. At the time, Bassett's was making 14 million allsorts a day at the Sheffield plant, all thanks to a fortunate slip from a fumbling sales rep.

What to eat and where to eat it

- **The Depot Eatery**

  Proudly curing, baking and making near enough everything that appears on the plate, The Depot Eatery on Burton Road is the perfect spot to get acquainted with Sheffield. Set in a cosy courtyard at the Neepsend side of Kelham Island, you will find eggs served on homemade bread along with a delicious list of sandwiches.

- **Granelli's**

  For old-fashioned spice at an old-fashioned price, head to Granelli's on Broad Street, where you will find a hearty selection of sweets measured out to order. Aniseed balls, bonfire toffee, liquorice torpedoes and, of course, liquorice allsorts line the shelves of this charming little shop.

- **Cutlery Works**

  In a city famous the world over for its knives and forks, it is apt to finish the day in a former cutlery works restored into one of the largest independent food halls in northern England. Try a Cuban sandwich from Rad Dude, a burger from Jimmy's or an onion bhaji wrap from Ma-Ba, among other things. Wash it down with a fresh craft beer from BoozeHound.

What to drink and where to drink it

- **Triple Point Brewery**

  For a badass brewery experience make your way to Triple Point Brewery, where wooden booths are arranged alongside a brewing gallery of shiny mash tuns, tanks and equipment. On hot days drinkers spill out into the courtyard, where a burger tent provides tasty sustenance.

- **Rutland Arms**

  Quirky, eclectic and a tad rebellious, the Rutland Arms is a well-regarded pub with a cleverly curated beer selection and a good food menu. 'Keg booze' and cask beers are chalked up on the bar and often include local beers from Blue Bee and Abbeydale breweries.

- **Kelham Island Tavern**

  If you are heading over to the Cutlery Works, consider factoring in a stop at Kelham Island Tavern too, where local beers from Blue Bee, Acorn, Barnsley Bitter and Bradfield have regular spots. Chunky pork pies are also often available with a sachet of brown sauce.

Shrewsbury Town

Fact box
Nickname – Salop
Colours – Blue and yellow
Ground – New Meadow
Built in – 2007
Capacity – 10,210

Introduction

Despite being one of England's oldest cheeses on record, mentioned in William the Conqueror's *Domesday Book* in 1086 and being proclaimed the best cheese in Europe by 16th-century historian John Speed, Cheshire cheese suffered a rather unfortunate decline over the last century, when it virtually became extinct. Today, one of the few dairies still making the crumbly and complex variety lies in the neighbouring county, Shropshire, where Appleby's produces some of the best cheeses in the land, according to cheesemonger and author Ned Palmer. The farm, located just outside the mediaeval town of Shrewsbury, uses unpasteurised milk from their own herd, set with animal rennet, bound in cloth and matured for between two and three months to make their traditional Cheshire, which has won countless awards, including the 'Gold' winner of the World Cheese Awards in 2018. Get your hands on some at one of the most alluring delis in the country, Appleyards, where you will be left drooling over its scrumptious window display of cheese and ale.

What to eat and where to eat it

- **Peaberry Grand Café**

  Find an inventive range of breakfast dishes at Peaberry Grand Café, where locally sourced ingredients feature heavily on the menu. Situated in the former Shearmen's Hall building in Milk Street, you will find produce from Corbetts of Shrewsbury in the 'our house all day' breakfast, with a range of flatbread lunches also available for those turning up a bit later.

- **Cook & Carve**

  Pack a mighty picnic with ingredients sourced from Shrewsbury Market Hall's premium delicatessen, with local farmhouse cheeses, Reg May's artisan pies, sausage rolls and veggie rolls using Shropshire cheese for you to enjoy.

- **Say Cheese**

  Purveyors of good-quality toasted sandwiches, Say Cheese is a Mecca for fans of the dairy treat, with cartoon mice and cheese grater lamps welcoming you in, along with the familiar smells of melted cheese on six-day sourdough bread. Try the 'shrews-brie' for something a little different or their signature 'easy cheesy'.

What to drink and where to drink it

- **Tap and Can**

  Those travelling by train should be prepared to be wowed twice in quick succession on arrival into Shrewsbury, first by the station's impressive architecture and secondly by the equally impressive selection of beers on offer at the Tap and Can across the road. With 14 beer lines and more than 100 cans and bottles, it's the perfect place to start after a long journey.

- **Loggerheads**

  Get a glimpse of Shrewsbury's mediaeval past in the Loggerheads pub, housed in a building that is thought to date back to 1665. Old Tudor buildings line Church Street, which has the feel of a film set. The pub has the same dated vibes with wooden pews, log fires and excellent ales, giving it plenty of pull power.

- **The Salopian Bar**

  Find beers from the Salopian Brewing Co., Stonehouse Brewery and Bathams at The Salopian Bar, a proud Shropshire establishment on the River Severn banks. A selection of Belgian beers can also often be found on draught, with a huge selection of bottles in reserve if not.

Southampton

Fact box
Nickname – The Saints
Colours – Red and white
Ground – St Mary's Stadium
Built in – 2000
Capacity – 32,384

Introduction

In 2016 the Juveniles restaurant in Paris witnessed a moment that would humble a nation of winemakers. In a blind tasting, French experts judged an English sparkling wine to be better than that of their own and, in doing so, announced on to the scene a new contender in a field that has almost exclusively been the preserve of Champagne for years. It was, as Matthew Jukes would note, quite 'immensely exciting', for in all his years never would he have believed that 'top French palates would take English sparkling wine for Champagne', yet after much development and favourable changes to the climate, it appeared that the time had finally arrived. Not that we should be too surprised. England's southern counties have a very similar terroir to the Champagne region, with chalk running under the Channel providing the perfect growing conditions for Chardonnay, Pinot Noir and Pinot Meunier on either side. But what Britain had lacked was the winemakers and expertise to do something about it, which is increasingly less of a concern. At the last count, close to 700 vineyards have cropped up in counties such as Kent,

Sussex and Hampshire, with some of the top viticulturists tending to them. As a result, occurrences such as the one in Paris are becoming increasingly frequent, and there is no better time to discover why than on a trip to The Solent.

What to eat and where to eat it

- **Docks Coffee**
  Day boats, passenger ferries and cruise liners all take moorings at Southampton's busy dockyards, home to much of the hustle and bustle in the city. A 'Docks big breakfast' will set you up for whatever your day has in store, with a full English breakfast, toast and preserves lined up next to a steaming mug of coffee.

- **The Oxford Brasserie**
  There's a lot to be happy with at The Oxford Brasserie by Queen's Park, but believe me, you haven't lived until you have tried their potted duck and orange paté. Served with a spiced date and prune chutney and toasted brioche, it is as heavenly a dish as you are likely to find this side of Paris.

- **Bacaro**
  An ever-changing menu of locally sourced, seasonal and fresh foods is offered at Bacaro, a small-plates-and-wine restaurant in Ironside House. The chic, industrial interior gives it a warm and relaxed atmosphere with exposed brick, beams and a pull-down paper board displaying daily specials.

What to drink and where to drink it

- **Dancing Man Brewery**

  Established in a striking old wool house, the Dancing Man Brewery retains much of its 14th-century charm with a warm, wood-and-stone-clad interior and a plaque outside commemorating its original usage. Today you can find eight cask pumps as well as almost a dozen intriguingly crafted cask taps that use knives, globes and spanners as leverage.

- **Duke of Wellington**

  Built in the 13th century and operating as a pub since 1494, the Duke of Wellington on Bugle Street is an old and creaky dark-timbered building that also happens to supply some of the best real ales on The Solent, mostly from Wadworth of Devizes.

- **Porters**

  Finish the day tucking into some of the best Champagne around at Porters, or if you fancy something with a touch more quality, they also serve English sparkling wine.

Southend United

Fact box
Nickname – The Shrimpers
Colours – Blue
Ground – Roots Hall
Built in – 1952
Capacity – 12,392

Introduction

Like most good ideas, the notion of Southend United was first dreamt up by a landlord and football enthusiasts in The Blue Boar pub in the early 1900s. The old public house, which still stands today just moments away from Roots Hall, sports a blue plaque on the wall to commemorate this fact and is very much in keeping with the typical pre-match pub fare. But for the best matchday experience, you need to be looking a few nautical miles down the estuary in the fisherman's hamlet of Leigh-on-Sea. Initially a shipbuilding town, Leigh grew thanks to its idyllic location at the foot of the Thames and morphed into a fishing village supplying the London market by road and barge. Today it houses seafood huts along the shore where punters queue up for lobster, crab, oysters, pickled herring, mussels, potted shrimp, cockles, winkles, smoked eel and more, before carrying it to the outdoor terrace to enjoy with a pint of local ale.

What to eat and where to eat it

- **Attic**

  Nothing kicks off a matchday at Roots Hall like a couple of 'Barling Beauties' at Southend's premier breakfast place. The locally sourced sausages are served up with rashers of sweet cured bacon and 'all the tea in China' at this sea-facing café, where a warm and jovial atmosphere will greet you away from the blustery chill of the nearby pier. Just up the road is Mawson's Micropub, which makes for a handy second stop once you've lined your stomach with a breakfast fit for kings.

- **Osborne Bros**

  Based on the shores of the Thames Estuary, Osborne Bros is a family-run café housed in 18th-century stable mews. Stocked with fresh produce from its fishmonger and cockle-processing factory down the road, the Osborne family operates two fishing vessels – *Mary Amelia* and *Renown* – which trawl the shallow waters using a dredge to dislodge the cockles. They can be enjoyed in the café alongside helpings of crab, oysters, shrimp and lashings of bread and butter.

- **The Pipe of Port**

  Formerly Davy's Wine Bar, The Pipe of Port was taken over in 1981 by two sisters with one husband in tow, and they went about preserving all that is good about a traditional, homely bistro. This philosophy remains today with homemade local food and an excellent array of wines served up in a relaxed and welcoming atmosphere that's a short walk from Roots Hall but far enough away to avoid the matchday rabble.

What to drink and where to drink it

- **West Road Tap**

  A worthy place for a pre-match pint, the West Road Tap is a cosy craft beer bar that boasts a wide selection of canned and draught ales. With local brews from Billericay Brewing Company, Bishop Nick and Leigh-on-Sea Brewery, it provides an intimate space to grab refreshments. But a word of warning: if you plan on drinking there after the match, beware the tide of home fans that will meet you en route.

- **Mawson's Micropub**

  Akin to stepping into someone's front room, Mawson's Micropub is a homely boozer that often serves more beers than it can accommodate punters. Nestled among a long row of terraced shop fronts, it offers a seamless transition from one of its many neighbouring greasy spoons into the pre-match drink mode. Along with local ales, you'll also find a selection of Belgian beers and cider.

- **The Crooked Billet**

  Offering unrivalled views across the cockle trawlers and sailing boats of Leigh Marsh, The Crooked Billet is an idyllic spot for an al fresco drink in the summer and a cosy traditional pub in which to snuggle up during the winter. With a special fish menu offering the likes of a 'soft-shell crab burger' and scallops paired with pork belly, it stays true to its locality. But Osborne Bros is just across the road if you prefer to pair your ale with cockles.

Stevenage

Introduction

You might think Stevenage FC, who have never recorded a league finish higher than sixth place in League One, have no business rubbing shoulders with the likes of Barcelona, Real Madrid and Manchester United, and on paper you'd be right. But in this part of Hertfordshire paper is of little worth. Matchday programmes are only available online and their most noteworthy sporting accomplishments were actually achieved on games consoles thanks to an ingenious marketing campaign rolled out by their sponsors, Burger King. Using FIFA 2020, they created several 'Stevenage Challenges' such as 'A Nutmeg for Nuggets' and 'Impossible for Impossible Whopper' to get e-gamers to share their goals on social media in exchange for food prizes, resulting in the club becoming the most popular team in the game. Tens of thousands of goals were uploaded, attracting hundreds of thousands of online views of their brand-sponsored kit, many more than they might expect to get in the 7,800-capacity Lamex Stadium.

What to eat and where to eat it

- **Duncan's**

  Using meat sourced directly from nearby Brookfield Farm on the outskirts of Stevenage, Duncan's full English is the perfect way to find your culinary feet in Hertfordshire. A circular chipolata sits coiled next to bacon, eggs, beans and hash browns, served with bottomless coffee.

- **Burger King**

  Visit Stevenage FC sponsors and the brand behind their FIFA fame at the Burger King in the Roaring Meg Retail Park. Try the plant-based 'Impossible Whopper' or the more meaty chicken nuggets to relive their e-sporting triumph.

- **Firejacks**

  Sauce lovers will feel very much at home at Firejacks steak and burger restaurant next to Stevenage train station. A sauce station consisting of every brand under the sun is organised from classic to fruity, barbecue, hot and extra hot.

What to drink and where to drink it

- **The Broken Seal**

  There will be no shortage of toilet humour at Stevenage's first-ever taproom to be found at the 'backside' of the high street on Basils Road. The Broken Seal serves beers from local microbrewery Bog Brew. Look out for Bomb's Away, Bottoms Up and Porter Potty.

- **Our Mutual Friend**

  Named after the famed Charles Dickens novel, Our Mutual Friend is an authentic ale pub based within a short walk of the Lamex Stadium. Find a good range of craft beers as well as a long list of cider and perry.

- **The Chequers Beer House**

  Serving up to ten cask ales from local brewers, The Chequers Beer House is an old pub sporting chic interior decor and a smart-looking beer garden at the back. Chequered tile flooring lines the ornate bar, with beers from Oakham Ales and Mad Squirrel often on tap.

Stoke City

Fact box
Nickname – The Potters
Colours – Red and white
Ground – bet365 Stadium
Built in – 1997
Capacity – 30,089

Introduction

For Staffordshire oatcakes, see Port Vale

Working life in industrial north Staffordshire was tough in the mid-19th century, when potters and colliers would earn a pittance and wives and families would be forced to get by on even less by the time the pub had received its share. To survive, many households would rely on lobby, a local dish that, as Marston's Pub catering development manager Ben Bartlett puts it, has no official recipe because it calls for whatever you have on hand to 'lob in' at the time. Much like lobscouse in Liverpool (see *Liverpool*), it is essentially a boiled-down stew using offal and gristle cuts of meat on offer at the butcher's. If you could get your hands on vegetables then potatoes and carrots might get thrown in to fill out the stew. If not, a generous dash of ale would be used to enhance the flavours, which would be in more abundant supply due to the low quality of the water in the area. Today Bartlett regards it as one of the best traditional dishes to pair with stout, especially on a cold rainy night in Stoke.

What to eat and where to eat it

- ### The Glost House
  Built in 1881 to satisfy the tremendous demand for majolica pottery, the Phoenix Works is an old Grade II-listed factory unit with a cobbled courtyard and iconic bottle oven. Stop off for refreshments at The Glost House, where you can enjoy an oatcake breakfast or a delicious 'egg in the hole'.

- ### Middleport Pottery
  Steeped in history, Middleport Pottery, described as 'model pottery' of the Staffordshire pottery industry at the time of its construction, is a working museum on the banks of the Trent and Mersey Canal. The old-school tea room serves local delicacies, including oatcakes and a delicious lobby served with a baguette.

- ### The Oatcake Boat
  The Oatcake Boat, or Boatcake if you will, is a café on a barge moored outside the bet365 Stadium serving up traditional Staffordshire treats for hungry football fans on matchdays. A double sausage and cheese oatcake wrap should keep your hunger at bay for at least 90 minutes and promises to be better than anything you'll find inside the stadium.

What to drink and where to drink it

- **The Lymestone Vaults**

  Start your day in Newcastle-under-Lyme at the brewery tap of Lymestone Brewery, where you will find a log-burning stoke, ten hand-pulled ales and a range of locally produced food that pairs perfectly with them. Craftily curated guest ales also make this a must-visit for all beer lovers.

- **The Strand**

  Find an ornate oak bar, chocolate-brown, buttoned-bench seating and a cosy fireplace at The Strand in Longton, a short walk from the local train station and with good accessibility to the bet365 Stadium. Based in an old jeweller's shop, the exterior has a mediaeval feel to it, with plenty of space inside, contrary to what you might first think.

- **The White Star**

  What better way to bid adieu to Stoke than with a homemade sausage roll and a pint of plum porter at The White Star pub, run by local brewers Titanic. Thick wedges of pastry-encrusted, seasoned pork are served with Branston pickle and mustard on a board fit for sharing, although you might want to be selfish.

Sunderland

Fact box
Nickname – The Black Cats
Colours – Red and white
Ground – Stadium of Light
Built in – 1997
Capacity – 49,000

Introduction

Ahead of Sunderland's first game at their new stadium in 1997, several names had been touted before then chairman Bob Murray finally landed on the Stadium of Light. Its proximity to the River Wear made 'Wearside Stadium' a natural choice. Others had suggested the 'New Roker Park', while a representative of the Labour government had even suggested it might be renamed after Diana, Princess of Wales, who died in the same year. In the end, Murray named it in honour of local miners who had worked for years in darkness, and the Davy lamp they carried with them as part of their working lives. He may also have been hinting at the nearby Souter Lighthouse which, when first lit in the 1870s, was described as 'without doubt one of the most powerful lights in the world'. Today you can enjoy a piping-hot panackelty in the café before indulging in a 'singin' hinnies', so named because they make a 'singing' sound while cooking, before the game, while taking in a view of the beautiful north-east coast.

What to eat and where to eat it

- **Souter Lighthouse**

  Take a trip along the coast to find a dish that warms the cockles like no other, in a historic lighthouse on Marsden Bay. Traditionally served with a stottie bun, panackelty is a hearty casserole dish that combines corned beef and root vegetables with potatoes, with plenty of warm juices for dipping. Finish the meal with a singin' hinnies scone to get a comprehensive taste of the north-east.

- **Fausto Coffee**

  Enjoy a 'pink slice' on Roker Beach at the vibey Fausto Coffee café. The local delicacy consists of jam sandwiched between two slices of shortbread which is then smothered with glowing pink icing. Best served with a warm mug of tea looking out over the marina.

- **Deli & Dips**

  Nothing will set you up for a long journey home quite like the 'saveloy dip', a regular feature in most chip shops across Sunderland. Take a bread bun, fill it with stuffing, pease pudding, sausage and mustard before dipping the whole thing in gravy. Wonderful!

What to drink and where to drink it

- **The Ship Isis**

  Like any good local pub, you will be left scratching your head for anything familiar when you first see the taps at The Ship Isis. Intriguing beer-pump clips immediately catch the eye, with several others dotted around the wall. A good selection of Belgian beers can also be found at this historic beer emporium.

- **The Dun Cow**

  Winner of two CAMRA Historic England Awards for best restoration and conservation, The Dun Cow is a Grade II-listed building with a listed back-bar fitting among other notable features. Beers served from seven hand-pulled taps often give precedence to north-east microbreweries, with the reformed Vaux Brewery a noteworthy pick.

- **Poetic Licence Bar**

  Home to the Poetic Licence Distillery, this trendy Roker bar is flush with local spirits and a range of craft keg beers from near and afar. Nine gins, including a Northern Dry, Baked Apple and Caramel, and a Fireside Spiced gin, are available to try, many of which go into alluring cocktail lists which get updated every month.

Swansea City

Introduction

For almost a century before Swansea City moved to the Liberty Stadium, the south Walian coastal outfit plied their trade at Vetch Field, named after a type of vegetable grown there at the time. The vetch, also known as the 'common vetch' or 'poor man's peas', is part of the legume family that includes some of the first domesticated crops eaten by humans. Today the old stadium has been transformed back into a community vegetable garden thanks to the Vetch Veg project spearheaded by residents of Sandfields and the artist Owen Griffiths. Together they created an 'urban utopia' in the city's centre where locals meet to tend their plots, swap recipes and share meals.

What to eat and where to eat it

- **Uplands Diner**

  Mention the Uplands Diner to any Swansea local and they will invariably associate it with one thing, the 'mega beast breakfast'. Comprised of ten rashers of bacon, eight sausages, five eggs and all the trimmings, the £13.25 stomach-stretcher will undoubtedly set you up for the day, with vast quantities of greasy goodness hemmed in by a wall of four slices of toast, four slices of bread and butter and four slices of fried bread.

- **BrewStone**

  BrewStone is a charming restaurant housed in a rustic, industrial setting in the heart of Uplands Swansea. It offers a wood-fire menu with a range of small pots available to share along with 'naked' fish and slow-cooked meats. The pizza menu is sublime, with the 'Cymru Am Byth' a must-try for travelling fans: Welsh rarebit sauce, smoked streaky bacon, buttered leeks and smoked cheese give you an authentic taste of Wales.

- **Pant-y-Gwydr**

  You will find some of the best lamb in Swansea at the French bistro Pant-y-Gwydr, where you can order a fillet served with an accompaniment of aubergine, courgette, pepper and dauphinoise potatoes; or 'gigot d'agneau confit, orge perlé', a slow-cooked leg of lamb with pearl barley, onions, carrots, garlic and red wine. Wash it down with a lovely bottle of Beaujolais.

What to drink and where to drink it

- **Boss Brewing Co.**

A stone's throw from the Liberty Stadium, craft beer brewery Boss has revolutionised matchday drinking for fans with a rustic taproom serving a range of award-winning ales. One of the few female-owned and -led breweries in the UK, it is a Mecca for comic book lovers, with many bold illustrations depicting the badass nature of the brewers. Try the Boss Boss, a 7.4 per cent Double IPA with a juicy but bold finish for the authentic feel.

- **BeerRiff Brewing Co.**

Take in views of the Swansea marina at the BeerRiff Brewing Co. taproom, with an extensive range of beers and access to a waterside beer garden on sunny days. The blue-clad building stretches over two floors, with its familiar lightning bolt logo emblazoned on the turret-shaped extension. Up to 15 beers can be found on tap on any given day, with a wide bottle and can range to choose from too.

- **No Sign Bar**

Regarded as Swansea's oldest pub, the No Sign Bar dates back to 1690. The name refers to the fact that it wasn't required to display a sign, like ordinary public houses, when it was first licensed as a wine bar. It was once frequented by the famous Welsh poet and writer Dylan Thomas. Today it houses four different bars, each with its own distinct character, although it still maintains a rustic character and wine focus.

**With thanks to SoS

Swindon Town

Fact box
Nickname – The Robins
Colours – Red
Ground – County Ground
Built in – 1890
Capacity – 15,728

Introduction

Pre-1840 very few people would have known about the small, sleepy hilltop town of Swindon. Its population numbered fewer than two thousand people, and other than the market or the occasional fair, there seemed to be little reason to bother with it, a point which is made clear in a 1798 copy of the *Salisbury and Winchester Journal*, which refers to Wroughton, which sits comfortably within the borough's boundaries today, as a village 'near Marlborough'. But that all changed with the arrival of Great Western Railway works, which soon transformed it into the home of one of the largest railway engineering complexes in the world, boosting its population considerably as people flocked to specially constructed villages that would house Turkish baths, swimming pools and even the first examples of a public library and comprehensive health service. What's more, the proliferation of thirsty workers played right into the hands of a certain Mr John Arkell, who had started a small-scale brewing business on a farm but soon switched to a more modern steam brewery when he found demand was far outstripping supply. By 1900,

THE GREAT PIE REVOLT

Arkell's owned more than a quarter of the pubs in the Swindon area and was firmly established as a cornerstone of life in the town, which was now almost unrecognisable from its humble status of 60 years before. It remains a big part of the town to this day as one of its oldest businesses and is still run by John Arkell's descendants, Nick, James, George and Alex Arkell.

What to eat and where to eat it

- ### Platform One Café
  Where better to start a day in a town that was revolutionised by the railways than in the STEAM Museum of the Great Western Railway? Grab a 'steamin' hot soup', 'stoker's hot sandwich' or a 'broad gauge burger' in the café above an impressive selection of locomotives.

- ### Los Gatos
  Prop up the bar for a spot of lunch at Swindon's premier tapas restaurant, Los Gatos. The busy, atmospheric establishment serves beautifully prepared dishes that crowd around cold cervezas. The black pudding with sweet red peppers and crisp, runny egg is exceptional.

- ### Harper's Steakhouse at the Weighbridge
  Another relic of Swindon's former rail days, Harper's Steakhouse at the Weighbridge is based in an old industrial weighing station for trains next to the West Coast Main Line. Once you finish admiring the building, you will find classic British cuisine with its own brewed beers inside. What's not to like?

What to drink and where to drink it

- **The Clifton**

  An Arkell's Brewery pub on the way out towards Wroughton, The Clifton is a spacious and happening pub that was a favourite among American GIs during the First World War. A big beer garden also has a street food stall where you can tuck into homemade burgers, hot dogs, pulled pork and hot pots.

- **The County Ground Hotel**

  For more of a matchday atmosphere, head to The County Ground Hotel behind the football ground's Town End side. Another Arkell's pub, you will find the classic 3B on tap, among other beers. Be warned, however, that it does get busy.

- **The Glue Pot**

  One of three Railway Village pubs built for workers but the only one still open, The Glue Pot dates back to the birth of Swindon's railway renaissance in 1850. Serving Hopback beers brewed just down the road in Salisbury, it is a quintessential, no-fuss real ale pub with a warm historic feel.

Tottenham Hotspur

Fact box
Nickname – The Lilywhites
Colours – White
Ground – Tottenham Hotspur Stadium
Built in – 2019
Capacity – 62,850

Introduction

By rights, Tottenham Hotspur's newly developed stadium is impressive enough to exclude them from these pages. Home to a cheese room, microbrewery and some of the best pie stands in the country, it is a defiant two fingers to the banal catering offering we revolters are trying to do away with. Open to punters for hours before and after the game and with good, local beers on tap and live music to keep you entertained, they certainly make a convincing argument for heading straight to the ground. But to do so would be to overlook the club's proud Jewish community and the food odyssey waiting to be discovered on its doorstep. It would mean missing out on salt beef and spicy courgettes, schnitzel sandwiches and delicious pastrami. You would forego the bagels adopted from Poland's Jewish communities, the smoked salmon brought over from Russia by Aaron Foreman (see *West Ham*) and the chance to try a spicy kishka stuffed in a capon. And you would miss the opportunity to experience a cuisine that has, as Claudia Roden notes in *The Book of Jewish Food*, 'adapted and adopted without ever losing its cultural identity', and in few places is that as evident as in north London. Fress!

What to eat and where to eat it

- **Blighty**

  Having served more than 200,000 English breakfasts since 2013, you can rest assured that the guys at Blighty know a thing or two about how to do a good one. Intensely orange Burford brown eggs are served with succulent smoked streaky bacon, Cumberland sausage, sautéed mushrooms, bone marrow, black pudding, tomatoes, beans and toast in what is undoubtedly one of the most refined fry-ups in London.

- **Deli Ninety Eight**

  Chow down on pulled beef, schnitzel and New York-style pastrami sandwiches at Deli Ninety Eight in south Tottenham. If you want to try something new, give the kishka a go. Stuffed in a capon, the spicy dish resembles the chicken Kiev in form, but certainly not in taste.

- **Monty's Deli**

  If your trip home means heading back via London, make sure to stop off at Monty's Deli to grab one of its famous sandwiches for the road. Widely regarded as being home to one of the best pastrami sandwiches in London, you will soon be in awe of the Reuben, which sees layers of meat stuffed inside rye bread with sauerkraut, mustard, Russian dressing and cheese layered on top.

What to drink and where to drink it

- **Beavertown**

  Founded in 2011 by the son of Led Zeppelin singer Robert Plant, Beavertown Brewery has become one of the nation's most-loved craft beers, with its Neck Oil and Gamma Ray now widely available in supermarkets and bars. A new brewery launched in 2020 has allowed it to increase capacity tenfold. You will find a fantastic taproom a short walk from the Tottenham Hotspur Stadium, where Beavertown beer can also be found on tap.

- **Redemption Brewing Company**

  Despite being dwarfed in size by its Beavertown counterparts, Redemption is, in fact, north London's oldest microbrewery and Tottenham's first in 100 years. It opens its small taproom for fans to enjoy the core range of IPAs, blondes and a 'Hotspur' amber ale on matchdays.

- **True Craft**

  The True Craft bar refurbished an old Victorian pub to give it a trendy, Shoreditch-style vibe. The outlet is on a mission to celebrate one of Britain's beer-brewing capitals, at least from a craft-brewing perspective, by showcasing brews from within the M25. You can be assured of provenance and a good, fresh-tasting beer in here.

Tranmere Rovers

Fact box
Nickname – Super White Army
Colours – White
Ground – Prenton Park
Built in – 1912
Capacity – 16,587

Introduction

Margarine and soap might not seem like typical bedfellows, but when the 'Unie' of Margarine Unie merged with the 'Lever' of soap makers Lever Brothers in 1929, they tied the knot on what would become one of the biggest consumer goods companies on the planet. Home to Lipton, Magnum, Ben & Jerry's, Hellmann's, Wall's, Pot Noodle and Colman's, to name but a few, Unilever has become a titan of industry, with an annual turnover in excess of 50 billion euros and with some 400 major brands in its stable. This astronomical growth is a far cry from its humble beginnings in the UK, when the sons of a small grocery business owner made their way down to Merseyside to manufacture their new free-lathering soap named 'Sunlight', made from glycerin and vegetable oils rather than tallow. The enterprising pair built a model village not unlike the one built for the workers of the Great Western Railway in Swindon (see *Swindon Town*) and set out to 'socialise and Christianise' business relations by investing profits back into the village in the shape of comfortable homes and healthy recreation activities. As

Lord Leverhulme told his workforce at the time, 'it would not do you much good if you send it down your throats in the form of bottles of whisky, bags of sweets, or fat geese at Christmas'. For those making their way over to Tranmere on Merseyrail, make sure to look out for Port Sunlight before feasting royally on its contraband treats.

What to eat and where to eat it

- **Caffé Cream**

  The first place to head to on arrival in Birkenhead is its illustrious park, which, as the locals will proudly tell you, influenced the design of Central Park in New York. You will get a good breakfast or perhaps even a sweet treat at Caffé Cream in the modern visitor centre, which is a short walk from Birkenhead Park station.

- **The Refreshment Rooms**

  A trip to Merseyside is not complete without trying Scouse (see *Everton*), and you will find an 'offensively good' one at riverside restaurant The Refreshment Rooms by Rock Ferry. Chunks of meat, root vegetables and onion are served in a rich gravy alongside a hunk of bread and homemade pickled cabbage. Wash down with a good local ale.

- **Zero Clucks Given**

  No chickens were harmed in the making of Birkenhead's first 100 per cent vegan junk food restaurant on Oxton Road. A stone's throw from the local Maccies, this place is living proof that vegan food does not have to be boring. Their 'mother clucker burger' beats a McChicken hands down any day of the week.

What to drink and where to drink it

- **Glen Affric Brewery**

  Housed on the River Mersey banks next to Birkenhead's historic shipyards, the Glen Affric Brewery is a modern addition to the quintessential heart of the Wirral Peninsula. There are commonly over 20 craft beers on at any one point, all of which can be enjoyed inside the brewery's modern industrial unit.

- **Peerless Brewing**

  Tangerine orange beer tanks greet you at Peerless Brewing, with an upstairs taproom serving good beers at a very reasonable price. The Jinja Ninja is a popular brew made with root ginger, chillies and lemons.

- **Bridge Inn**

  A short walk from Port Sunlight train station to the Bridge Inn will give you a good feel for the model village built by the Lever Brothers for their workforce in the late 19th century. The registered conservation area contains some 900 Grade II-listed buildings along with bowling greens and other such recreational areas.

Walsall

Fact box
Nickname – The Saddlers
Colours – Red
Ground – Bescot Stadium
Built in – 1990
Capacity – 11,300

Introduction

'Richard James AKA Grorty Dick is a present-day Faggot Pioneer,' the author profile of his book, *The Good Faggot Guide*, notes. Quite remarkably, there is nothing offensive in that sentence. Grorty Dick is a classic Black Country pudding made from soaked groats, beef, leeks, onion and beef stock, while faggots are also a local delicacy that are comprised of pork off-cuts and offal wrapped in a coat of breadcrumbs and onions and served with mushy peas, mash and gravy. According to James's book, which was launched in a bid to save the traditional Brummie dish, the Midlands staple gained popularity due to the prevalence of backyard pigs in the city, which would be fattened up with pigswill until they were big enough for slaughter. At that point, nothing of its carcass would be wasted. The blood was caught and made into black pudding, ears were stuffed and eaten, and even the bladder would be used to cover jars or be turned into a football. The caul, liver, kidney and even the fry would be either baked or used for faggots in what was a long, painstaking process. They are cooked in gravy and served with mooshay pays.

What to eat and where to eat it

- **Jack & Ada's Café Restaurant**

  Follow your nose off the bus or out of the train station and you will end up at Jack & Ada's Café Restaurant, where enticing aromas of sausage and bacon welcome travellers to the market town. The full English is piled high with black pudding, hash browns, sausage, bacon and eggs. A generous helping of toast is served on the side.

- **The Black Country Arms**

  Grab yourself a hearty plate of pork faggots in rich onion gravy served with chips and mooshay pays at The Black Country Arms. It pairs perfectly with an amber ale from the pub's namesake brewery.

- **Five Rivers À La Carte**

  Expect some pretty special Indian cuisine at Five Rivers À La Carte, where chef Rashpal Sunner has created an innovative and exciting gourmet food menu. The sophisticated, split-level restaurant is well regarded locally and a visit is an idyllic way to end the day.

What to drink and where to drink it

- **AJ's Ales Brewery**

  Brewed in the heart of Walsall, you don't get beer much fresher than that served in AJ's Ales Brewery. A core range of SPA, best bitter and ruby is complemented with a special 'stuck' range to suit tastes or circumstance. Will you be stuck in the mud, stuck on blondes or stuck in the dog house?

- **The Pretty Bricks**

  A Black Country Ales pub, The Pretty Bricks is an old-fashioned boozer with a roaring coal fire and cosy saloon, rear lounge and snug. Regular beers include Bradley's Finest Golden, Fireside and Pig on the Wall, with guest ales chalked up.

- **The Victoria**

  Dating back to the mid-19th century, The Victoria is a small pub on Lower Rushall Street serving beers from Wye Valley, Banks's Brewery and Church End Brewery, among others. A small bar room welcomes you in, with a larger room at the back and a room upstairs with a pool table.

Watford

Fact box
Nickname – The Hornets
Colours – Yellow and black
Ground – Vicarage Road
Built in – 1922
Capacity – 22,220

Introduction

Despite having a solid beer heritage, there are 'disappointingly few proper pubs close to the stadium', *Golden Pages* fanzine editor Tom Wicks tells me ahead of a visit to the Hertfordshire town. Once associated with the Benskins brewery, which purchased Vicarage Road in 1921 and leased it to the club at a peppercorn rent, the club was nicknamed 'The Brewers' before adopting The Hornets in 1959 in a nod to the new kit. Today Watford lives in comparative beer wilderness, which has seen the popular Watford supporters' group, The 1881 Movement, set up their own 'bunker' near the Rookery Stand serving beer from the local Mad Squirrel brewery. Covered in club paraphernalia, it has become quite the hit on matchdays and is well worth a visit – if you can get in.

What to eat and where to eat it

- **Fry Days**

  Place your bets and grab your chips at one of Vicarage Road's most popular matchday haunts. A big hit with the locals, Fry Days is an ideally placed chippy that intersects most routes down to the stadium from both main train stations and the town centre. Take your pick of fish and chips, burgers and pies, with the 'masala codfish' well worthy of a try – a British Asian fusion with some kick.

- **ZINCO**

  A popular haunt of the Watford players, ZINCO is an independent Italian restaurant located in the heart of the town's pedestrianised entertainment district. With a wide selection of authentic dishes to choose from, it is widely revered as one of the best restaurants in town, boasting a range of speciality and traditional pasta dishes that are highly rated. In the summer months, you can dine al fresco in the heart of the street, kicking back with a spritz under the shaded parasols.

- **Nana's Lebanese Restaurant**

  Small, unpretentious and unassuming, Nana's is the perfect spot for a post-match meal, offering a range of Lebanese food from small mezze dishes to 'meshwi' (mixed meats) off the grill, and traditional sweet pastries. Known for its warm hospitality, there is always a jovial atmosphere that is made all the more cheerful by the fact that it is bring your own booze. You may even be treated to Arabic belly dancing if you time your visit well.

What to drink and where to drink it

- **Nascot Arms**

  Tucked away from the hustle and bustle of the town on a charming residential street, the Nascot Arms is a nice spot for those who enjoy a quiet pint before the game in a more peaceful setting. Once a Benskins pub, it still, until recently, carried the branding of the now-defunct brewery. You will find Greene King cask ales along with some impressive guest ales too.

- **The Villiers Arms**

  Stepping inside is like taking a step back in time, with a cosy and warm interior peppered with old advertisements and decorations, giving it a museum-like feel. A coal fire will burn on cold winter days and you can be sure of a small crowd outside in the summer. Jump off the train at Bushey if travelling on the Overground on certain trains. It is a short walk to the ground from there.

- **The Oddfellows**

  Drink and be merry in Watford's token Irish pub, just moments away from Vicarage Road. Occupying the space of three former terraced houses, The Oddfellows feels at home in its surroundings, wedged between its neighbours on Fearnley Street. A warm welcome is extended to both home and away fans on matchdays, when an outside bar operates alongside a catering area offering classic burgers, posh dogs and chilli dogs off the grill.

* With thanks to the *Golden Pages*

West Bromwich Albion

Introduction

Pound for pound, there is not much that sets West Bromwich apart on the culinary front, except for the fact that when the club was first founded in 1878 most of its players earned their crust by making traditional weighing scales at the local spring works. Known back then as the West Bromwich Strollers because they had to walk to nearby Wednesbury to buy a football, the club relied on 'pocket steelyard' cricketers looking for a winter sport in the early days. Along with kitchen scales and classic spring balances, they also produced irons, mincers, potato chippers and the first typewriters made in the UK at the local factory. A year later, the team became the first to adopt the Albion suffix, after the district where several players lived or worked, close to what is today Greets Green.

What to eat and where to eat it

- **Harry's Diner**

  Head down to Harry's for a 'monster breakfast' to get the day off to a bumper start. Full breakfast mashings fill an oversized plate, with toast on the side. A coffee and a newspaper will still give you change out of a tenner.

- **The Vine**

  Experience the delights of an Indian BBQ at The Vine, where the succulent aromas of spiced meats waft from an open grill. Charred chicken tikka, spicy pork steak and tilapia fish are the picks of the options, all of which pair nicely with an icy cold beer.

- **Turquoise Kitchen & Bar**

  Often overlooked by tourists, Turkey's south-eastern region is a gastronomic marvel waiting to be discovered. Home to a huge diversity of cultures and cuisines, the Silk Road influences have created dishes unlike anywhere else in the world, many of which can be sampled at the Turquoise Kitchen & Bar in the form of charcoal-grilled kebabs, tasty mezzes and sweet pastries.

What to drink and where to drink it

- **The Old Hop Pole**

West Brom memorabilia abounds in The Old Hop Pole, where a central bar straddles two rooms, a cosy log fire burns in the winter and a small beer garden welcomes punters in the summer. Expect a good rotation of beers, with local ales from Shropshire, Yorkshire and the Midlands regularly on tap.

- **The Wheatsheaf**

Black and white to its core, not only does The Wheatsheaf sport the local football team's colours on its exterior, it has even tiled the male toilets in the same style. Black Country bitter, Black Country lager and even Black Country pork scratchings can be had in this proud pub, all at a reasonable price.

- **The Cricketers Arms**

Pay homage to Albion's cricketing converts at this pub-cum-steakhouse, which houses a giant wall painting of a middle stump being skittled and on its side. Tuck yourself into a private booth with a screen, a beer and a steak as you analyse and unpack the day's action.

West Ham United

Fact box
Nickname – The Irons
Colours – Claret and blue
Ground – London Stadium
Built in – 2011
Capacity – 60,000

Introduction

Before West Ham upped sticks and moved to the commercial magnet that is the Olympic Park, I would have had few gripes about eating and drinking around the authentically East End area of Upton Park. On most matchdays, Green Street would be abuzz with people getting their pre-match fix from Nathan's Pie and Eels or the Rib Man of West Ham, maker of the famous Holy F*ck sauce. But as one stall owner said ahead of the move, these places were never going to get a look-in at the newly built corporate-fest that became London Stadium. Today you'll find chain restaurants and bars clustered around the renovated park, which sent some 300 firms of the Lower Lea Valley packing when the Olympics arrived in 2012. Thankfully many still exist today for those minded to seek them out, displaced but not forgotten.

What to eat and where to eat it

- **The Rib Man**

  An institution at West Ham's old Boleyn Ground, Mark Gevaux, otherwise known as 'The Rib Man' or even the 'King of Ribs', has been serving up his succulent baby-back pork ribs for years. A fanatic Hammers fan, he closes shop when he sells out, allowing time for him to join his punters at the game.

- **H. Forman & Son**

  Formerly located in the middle of the Olympic Stadium, H. Forman & Son is a factory-cum-restaurant specialising in the centuries-old 'London cure' method of smoking fish. Although it is widely believed that smoked salmon comes from Scotland, that is not strictly true: the salmon may be from Scottish waters, but the smoke is from London. Today you can taste old ways of preserving fish, brought over by Jewish immigrants, in Forman's Restaurant overlooking the stadium which replaced its first home.

- **BJ's Pie & Mash Shop**

  A trip to these parts is not complete without a round of pie, mash and liquor at a proper East End shop, and while BJ's may feel small, it is all the better for it. Get involved in some good old rhyming slang and Cockney banter as you tuck into your lunch, and try the stewed eels if you're brave enough.

What to drink and where to drink it

- **CRATE Brewery**

  Get a feel for East London as it was at CRATE Brewery, providing canal-side craft beer and pizza in an old factory in the former industrial heartlands. A short walk down the River Lee Navigation will get you to the London Stadium, where you can feel glad of eschewing the ground's mainstream catering fare.

- **Howling Hops Brewery and Tank Bar**

  Take a pew at one of Howling Hops's long classroom tables to enjoy its range of beers served straight from shiny tanks behind the bar. Inspired by similar movements in the Czech Republic, the direct tank-to-glass approach allows for a wonderful unpasteurised, unfiltered taste.

- **Beer Merchants Tap**

  Home to London's only dedicated sour beer blender, the Beer Merchants Tap is an innovative and adventurous brewery that will certainly keep you guessing. The taproom features 20 key lines, two cask handpulls and more than 600 different bottles and cans, teeing you up for an intriguing session.

Wigan Athletic

Fact box
Nickname – The Latics
Colours – Blue and white
Ground – DW Stadium
Built in – 1999
Capacity – 25,133

Introduction

The history of Wigan Athletic Football Club starts in earnest with one man. After suffering a horrific leg break in the 1960 FA Cup Final, David Whelan opened a stall on Wigan market where he revealed an entrepreneurial flair that would see him go on to spearhead one of Britain's most prominent sports retailers. Today, playing under his initials, the club pays homage to his input after Whelan took them from a Division Four side to a Premier League outfit with an estimated investment of £100 million. Part of that could well have come from a local pie venture, Poole's Pies, which he sold for £5 million in 2012. Yet, despite the town's proud pie heritage and a club mascot dressed as a pie, you won't find any of the local suppliers on sale at the DW, much to the chagrin of local supporters. To get a taste of the town, you'll have to make a pit stop before kick-off.

What to eat and where to eat it

- **The Trawlerman Fish & Chip Shop**

  Wigan kebab, smack barm, pey wet and 'Babby's yed' are just some of the delights on offer at this fish and chip institution in Wigan's west end. The foremost delicacy is renowned in the local area and comprises a buttered barm with a meat and potato pie. So popular is this carb-loading food staple it even has its own Facebook page. Also, don't shy away from a smack barm with pey wet (pea sauce) before taking a short stroll down the river to the DW.

- **Galloways Pies**

  Founded in 1971 by Ronald and Patricia Galloway, the Galloway's chain of bakeries has grown from a lone outlet in Pemberton to 23 shops across the north-west. The first café still stands proudly less than a 30-minute stroll from the DW, where you can get a pre-match fill of the 'quintessential Wigan' meat and potato pie as well as staggis (steak and haggis) and blaggis (black pudding and haggis) pies, which are made using meat supplied by the local butcher, H. Greaves & Son of Skelmersdale.

- **Pepper Lane Pie Shop**

  Considered Wigan's best-kept secret by all those who dine there, Pepper Lane Pie Shop is a small out-of-town outlet that is more than worth the journey. Formally known as Gents, the bakery serves up pies that require two hands to eat and use proper meat sauce and real chunks of steak rather than the minced, bland fillings we have become accustomed to. Pie aficionados should consider it a pilgrimage, and for those less devoted, perhaps this will convert them?

What to drink and where to drink it

- ### Wigan Central

  Train enthusiasts will delight in this pub, which pays homage to the old Wigan Central railway station, replaced 50 years ago with Wallgate and North Western. Fitted out in the style of a railway waiting room, it has three booths reminiscent of the old carriage seating, and a converted train carriage bar stacked with real craft ales and ciders. A selection of pork pies, cheese and Scotch eggs are also available from the snack board.

- ### Tap 'n' Barrel

  Sample Wigan's most local beer in the Tap 'n' Barrel, a micropub set up by the founders of Martland Mill Brewery in the town centre. Nestled among the independent shops and cafés of Jaxons Court, the intimate setting compliments a rich sense of locality as you prop up the high-top counter or huddle around stools outside. A pint of Chonkin Feckle is a fine way to kick the day off, but be sure to sample the Arctic Convoy if you hit it on the way home.

- ### John Bull Chop House

  Historic pubs are hard to come by in Wigan, but at 500 years old, John Bull Chop House certainly fits the bill. Situated in the town's only conservation area, with a whitewashed exterior and a warm interior with exposed wooden pillars, the pub is one of the few surviving examples of courtyard development in the town. Today some 17 draught beers are on show, including six cask ales which change with the seasons. It also has pool and table football tables.

Wolverhampton Wanderers

> **Fact box**
> Nickname – Wolves
> Colours – Amber and black
> Ground – Molineux Stadium
> Built in – 1889
> Capacity – 32,050

Introduction

If you consider Wolverhampton's A4150 ring road to be the face of a clock, then everything worth knowing about for travelling football fans is located between the hours of ten and two. At one end is the train station, a major hub providing access to most parts of the country, and at the other is Banks's Brewery, with Molineux slap bang in the middle. Within these four 'hours' you can learn more about the city than in the other eight combined. You will find the historic St. Peter's Church dating back to the 15th century, the Civic Hall where Nirvana performed 'All Apologies' for the first time before a live audience in 1991, the Grand Theatre and, of course, the historic old parks bought by local merchant Benjamin Molineux in 1744, which now play host to the Wanderers. But there is only one way to get right to the heart of Wolverhampton and understand its place in the Black Country, and that's to try a pint of Banks's Dark Mild. As the brewery says, 'this is pure Black Country stuff. No one in the world could do it like us.'

What to eat and where to eat it

- **Lindy Lou's Café and Coffee Shop**

  Occupying one of Wolverhampton's most iconic buildings which dates back to the 1600s, Lindy Lou's Café and Coffee Shop has passed through many hands before it was turned into a breakfast spot in 2017. Formerly a baker, toy shop, store and welfare centre, the timber-framed building has a rich and varied past, with an excellent breakfast to be had in there these days.

- **The Grain Store**

  Head to the historic King Street to get a taste of Wolverhampton's industrial past at The Grain Store, a gin emporium and kitchen. The lunch menu features a wide range of gin-inspired concoctions, including gin and tonic battered fish and chips and 'G&T fish fingers', all of which pair perfectly with a wide range of gins behind the bar.

- **Café Maxsim**

  A BYOB tapas restaurant in the heart of the city centre, Café Maxsim is a small restaurant with an impressive selection of dishes from over eight exotic countries, including Italy, Greece, Egypt, Mexico and Spain. There is a great 'secret garden' at the rear for those who enjoy al fresco dining.

What to drink and where to drink it

- **Banks's Brewery**

  Take a tour around Banks's Brewery to discover the secret behind the brewer's historic cask ales. The tour finishes in the bar, where you can sample the full range of beer. Make it half a dark if you want the authentic Midlands experience.

- **The Combermere Arms**

  Tucked away in Chapel Ash and within a few minutes' walk of Molineux Stadium is The Combermere Arms, a quirky real ale pub with bags of character. You will find a handful of small rooms with cosy fireplaces inside and a generously-sized beer garden at the back. If you are lucky, there might even be a pie, sausage and cheese-tasting festival on.

- **The Lych Gate Tavern**

  Serving the full range from Black Country Ales, The Lych Gate Tavern is a historic boozer next to St. Peter's Church, with a red-brick exterior and wooden-beam ceiling giving it a warm and historic feel. Expect beers from nearby Shropshire, Nottinghamshire and Birmingham to be chalked up too.

Wycombe Wanderers

> **Fact box**
> Nickname – The Chairboys
> Colours – Navy and pale blue
> Ground – Adams Park
> Built in – 1990
> Capacity – 10,137

Introduction

Public scrutiny of the traditional branches of government has always been of utmost importance to the basic functioning of a democracy. In Britain, there were always three 'estates' made up of the commoners, the nobility and the clergy. The press – the so-called 'fourth estate' – acts as a critical and indispensable check on all three and, for Sir Edmund Burke, is the 'most important of them all', for without it, we would have no way of keeping the powers that be in check. But long before the Right Honourable member came out in defence of a free press the good people of High Wycombe had come up with a different way of scrutinising their local politicians – they weighed them. The tradition, which dates back to 1678, would be carried out at the beginning and end of each year of service to see if the mayor had been piling on the pounds at the taxpayer's expense. The custom has survived to the present day when the old hanging scales are rolled out and the town crier announces, 'And no more!' if the mayor has not gained weight, or 'And some more!' if they have. Thankfully they are now spared being pelted with tomatoes and rotten fruit in the event of any weight gain, which is more than can be said for the poor representatives in the years gone by.

What to eat and where to eat it

- **The Works**

  In a town that takes a dim view of overindulgence, The Works sticks two fingers up to convention with an American savoury-meets-sweet themed menu that will leave both you and the town crier shouting, 'And some more!' A loaded waffle breakfast is a good way to start the day. Options include eggs royale, huevos rancheros and a half English.

- **The Apple Orchard**

  A short walk away from Wycombe Wanderers' out-of-town stadium, The Apple Orchard is a rural gem nestled in the rolling Chiltern Hills. Grab a sandwich or a bagel before the game to be enjoyed in their rustic 17th-century building.

- **Heidrun**

  Marrying craft beer with delicious food pairings, the Norse-inspired Heidrun on Paul's Row is a modern eatery focused around a wrap-around bar with 20 ever-changing beer and cider taps. Small plates such as BBQ pork belly bites, jalapeño poppers and a black pudding Scotch egg are all perfect with a pint.

What to drink and where to drink it

- **Mad Squirrel Tap & Bottle Shop**

  Right in the heart of High Wycombe, the Mad Squirrel's taproom features up to 20 taps of craft beer, with a pizza kitchen on site to keep the beer munchies at bay. There is a secret roof terrace at the top on hot or dry days, which makes for a rather nice beer haven.

- **Chiltern Taps**

  A sports and craft beer bar next to the Eden Shopping Centre, the Chiltern Taps is one of those bars often humorously referred to as a 'husband day care'. With a dozen screens, at least as many beer taps and a good pub grub menu, you can happily while away the hours in here.

- **The Belle Vue**

  A real ale boozer next to the Chiltern Main Line, The Belle Vue is a good, honest pub featuring local beers amid a sea of clips and tankards dotted around the bar. A central fire keeps things cosy in the winter, while a small beer garden can be found at the back in the summer months.